2 **3** 4 5 6 7 8 9 10

THE TECH SET

Ellyssa Kroski, Series Editor

Microblogging and Lifestreaming in Libraries

Robin M. Hastings

lita

Neal-Schuman Publishers, Inc.

New York   London

Published by Neal-Schuman Publishers, Inc.
100 William St., Suite 2004
New York, NY 10038

Published in cooperation with the Library Information and Technology
Association, a division of the American Library Association.

Printed and bound in the United States of America.

The paper used in this publication meets the minimum requirements of
American National Standard for Information Sciences—Permanence of
Paper for Printed Library Materials, ANSI Z39.48-1992.

ISBN: 978-1-55570-707-1

CONTENTS

Don't miss this book's companion wiki and podcast!

Turn the page for details.

THE TECH SET is more than the book you're holding!

All 10 titles in THE TECH SET series feature three components:

1. the book you're now holding;
2. companion wikis to provide even more details on the topic and keep our coverage of this topic up-to-date; and
3. author podcasts that will extend your knowledge and let you get to know the author even better.

The companion wikis and podcasts can be found at:

techset.wetpaint.com

At **techset.wetpaint.com** you'll be able to go far beyond the printed pages you're now holding and:

▶ access regular updates from each author that are packed with new advice and recommended resources;
▶ use the wiki's forum to interact, ask questions, and share advice with the authors and your LIS peers; and
▶ hear these gurus' own words when you listen to THE TECH SET podcasts.

To receive regular updates about TECH SET technologies and authors, sign up for THE TECH SET Facebook page (**facebook.com/nealschumanpub**) and Twitter (**twitter.com/nealschumanpub**).

For more information on THE TECH SET series and the individual titles, visit **www.neal-schuman.com/techset**.

▶

FOREWORD

Welcome to volume 3 of The Tech Set.

Microblogging and Lifestreaming in Libraries is a start-to-finish passport to using such services as Twitter, Friendfeed, and Tumblr to engage and communicate with library patrons. Veteran microblogger Robin Hastings leads readers through how to use these cutting-edge social media applications to keep patrons updated, market the library, and build community. This comprehensive field guide covers everything from how to feed blog posts into Twitter, feed tweets into a Web site, and utilize Twitter for library events, to ways to incorporate these tools into your organization's marketing strategy.

The idea for The Tech Set book series developed because I perceived a need for a set of practical guidebooks for using today's cutting-edge technologies specifically within libraries. When I give talks and teach courses, what I hear most from librarians who are interested in implementing these new tools in their organizations are questions on how exactly to go about doing it. A lot has been written about the benefits of these new 2.0 social media tools, and at this point librarians are intrigued but they oftentimes don't know where to start.

I envisioned a series of books that would offer accessible, practical information and would encapsulate the spirit of a 23 Things program but go a step further—to teach librarians not only how to use these programs as individual users but also how to plan and implement particular types of library services using them. I thought it was important to discuss the entire life cycle of these initiatives, including everything from what it takes to plan, strategize, and gain buy-in, to how to develop and implement, to how to market and measure the success of these projects. I also wanted them to incorporate a broad range of project ideas and instructions.

Each of the ten books in The Tech Set series was written with this format in mind. Throughout the series, the "Implementation" chapters, chock-full of detailed project instructions, will be of major interest to all readers. These chapters start off with a basic "recipe" for how to effectively use the technology in a library, and then build on that foundation to offer more and more advanced project ideas. I believe that readers of all levels of expertise will find something useful here as the proposed projects and initiatives run the gamut from the basic to the cutting-edge.

I had the chance to interview Robin Hastings in spring 2008 about the innovative ways she was using Twitter at the Missouri River Regional Library. During the process I learned that Robin is one of those people who just "gets it"—she is incredibly savvy about the latest social media technology and can translate that knowledge into concrete strategies for using those tools in libraries. If you're contemplating a microblogging or lifestreaming initiative in your library, you'll want to consult this book.

Ellyssa Kroski
Information Services Technologist
Barnard College Library
www.ellyssakroski.com
http://oedb.org/blogs/ilibrarian
ellyssakroski@yahoo.com

Ellyssa Kroski is an Information Services Technologist at Barnard College as well as a writer, educator, and international conference speaker. She is an adjunct faculty member at Long Island University, Pratt Institute, and San Jose State University where she teaches LIS students about emerging technologies. Her book *Web 2.0 for Librarians and Information Professionals* was published in February 2008, and she is the creator and Series Editor for The Tech Set 10-volume book series. She blogs at iLibrarian and writes a column called "Stacking the Tech" for *Library Journal*'s Academic Newswire.

PREFACE

What are you doing *right* now? This is the fundamental question that drives microblogging and lifestreaming Web 2.0 applications. The most advanced libraries in the world are utilizing Web instant notification services to communicate with patrons, staff, and other libraries about news that is happening now. Staying informed with up-to-the-second information allows for maximum efficiency and streamlined productivity, goals for libraries navigating today's Web 2.0 universe.

Simply put, *Microblogging and Lifestreaming in Libraries* begins by defining the characteristics of microblogging and lifestreaming applications, followed by ways for all librarians to plan and implement them at your libraries. The purpose of microblogging (micro-Web-logging) is instant communication via short written messages or blogs, which are then posted publicly on the Web, sent through an Instant Message (IM) service, sent to a desktop application or e-mail, and/or texted to your cell phone. The true power of this form of communication comes from the ability to send your message through one or all of these outlets at the same time, allowing for maximum visibility. With microblogging, if your library needs to quickly get out the message that it will be closed because of a water main break, everyone, everywhere, will know. Lifestreaming applications (also referred to as "social aggregators") combine status updates (microblogs from various applications) into one interface. Lifestreaming applications not only allow you to view all of your social activities in one spot and with one interface, but they also allow you to follow and view other users and their updates from the services they share on the aggregator's site.

Libraries use Twitter and other microblogging applications like Tumblr and lifestreaming applications like FriendFeed every day to reach out to their patrons, donors, and elected officials to get information and advocacy materials out fast. Other libraries use it to get the word out about just how great they are! Still others use it to announce library programs and special events or just to converse with patrons in an incredibly cost-effective way.

▶ ORGANIZATION AND AUDIENCE

Twitter, Plurk, Identi.ca, and Yammer are all Web 2.0 applications that enable users to communicate with each other in a short, concise way. For those who are unfamiliar with these services, the first chapters that follow explain what they do, how to set up an account, and then how to use them. Subsequent chapters cover how to integrate your microblogging and other social networking services (such as Facebook) into one lifestreaming interface.

Chapter 1 introduces today's current microblogging and lifestreaming applications and helps you determine which are right for your library. Chapter 2 assists you in setting up a plan for implementing the appropriate applications, including how to convince resistant staff and how to create new user accounts. Chapter 3 describes the step-by-step process for implementing your plans. Chapter 4 discusses marketing and ways to get the word out. Chapter 5 highlights microblogging and lifestreaming best practices, and Chapter 6 covers how to measure and quantify the success of your implementation efforts. A "Recommended Resources" chapter provides excellent supplemental information for those still wanting to learn more about these technologies.

To those that haven't used them, these services seem trivial for library applications. Many people, when first presented with the idea of Twitter—or any other microblogging or lifestreaming application—feel that it is silly and not appropriate for professional work applications. *Microblogging and Lifestreaming in Libraries* will guide you on how to communicate the tremendous potential of these services for enhancing user services and then outline the

most effective and professional way to put your library at the fore-
front of library Web 2.0 communication.

►1

INTRODUCTION: MICROBLOGGING AND LIFESTREAMING BASICS

► **Definitions and Characteristics**
► **Choosing Your Service**

► DEFINITIONS AND CHARACTERISTICS

Microblogging is text messaging on steroids. It is, essentially, the practice of making very short, bloglike posts that are broadcast out to anyone who has signed up to receive them. The most popular microblogging service, Twitter (www.twitter.com), has a limit of 140 characters for each post to the service. This limit makes Twitter ideal for many different short, instant update applications—including cell phone text messaging and Instant Messaging as well as the horde of different desktop applications and Web-based mashups that exist out there today. Twitter's single question, posted above the text entry box on each person's account, is "What are you doing now?" Answering this question sends a status update to Twitter, to be delivered to your "tweeps," and can be done through any of the Twitter clients, which let you read and write the microblog posts that are called "tweets." There are also third-party desktop applications that will display all of the information available through the Twitter Web site on your computer's desktop—without requiring you to have a browser window open to keep track of the conversation.

Tweet: A 140-character post to the microblogging service called Twitter, a status update to the Twitter service.

Tweople: People who use the Twitter service.

Tweeps: Your friends who are also on Twitter.

Tweetup: A physical meeting of tweeps, arranged via Twitter.

After answering Twitter's simple question about what you are doing "right now," your tweet (your answer) is then posted to let your followers (people who have signed up to get your tweets) know what is going on in your life right now. This is where the fact that your Twitter status posts are easily updated and read by a simple, non-Internet-connected cell phone becomes important. An Internet connection is not necessary to update your followers about what you are doing—just your ability to send a text message to the Twitter service will do! People can update their accounts and let their friends and followers know what they are doing while standing in line, attending a program at the library, or just about anywhere. If there is cell phone service (and, as of this writing, you are in the United States, because the cell phone features are limited to just the United States), there is an opportunity to connect with Twitter.

Twitter is not the only microblogging service available, although it does get the most press. Plurk (www.plurk.com) offers the same services as Twitter but adds a few extras. The posts to Plurk are placed on a horizontal timeline, rather than in chronological order down a page, so that you can get an idea of what your friends on Plurk are doing horizontally rather than vertically. Plurk also offers "karma points"—the more posts you make and the more friends you have, the more points you can earn. Points can be earned by posting to Plurk, updating your profile, getting responses from other Plurkers to your posts on Plurk, and inviting your real-life friends to join the service. Karma points give you access to more emoticons to use in your posts, let you change your display name, and permit you to give your own title to your personal Plurk timeline.

Identi.ca (http://identi.ca) is another microblogging alternative to Twitter. Identi.ca uses the open source software StatusNet (http://status.net) to run a service similar but not identical to Twitter. There are a few differences. Identi.ca makes groups easy and obvious to use, while Twitter's grouping features are almost an afterthought and difficult to find from the Twitter homepage. The main benefit to Identi.ca is that the software it is running on is available to the public for use; if the Identi.ca site dies, users can still have access to the platform on which it runs. If you are comfortable running this kind of application on your own server, you can create an entirely in-house version of Twitter.

There are "enterprise" microblogging services out there, too. Yammer (www.yammer.com) lets you create a private network available only to people within your company or organization. This is a nice feature for managers who want to give employees the sense of networking with each other—without worrying about an employee disclosing sensitive data through a posting to one of the more public microblogging systems. Yammer is directly modeled on the Twitter format—SMS (Short Message Service), IM, and Web connections are all available—but the Yammer service stresses privacy and data control in ways that the public services cannot. Yammer carries all posts over the Internet via SSL (Secure Socket Layer) so that all posts are encrypted and secure from prying eyes. All posts are archived, as well, giving the organization a way to easily find information that might have been "yammered" about on the service over time.

All of these microblogging services do one thing only—they provide a way for their users to communicate with other users of

Popular Microblogging and Lifestreaming Services

Twitter
www.twitter.com
Launched in March 2006

Plurk
www.plurk.com
Launched in June 2008

Identi.ca
http://identi.ca
Launched in July 2008

Yammer
www.yammer.com
Launched in September 2008

FriendFeed
http://friendfeed.com
Launched in October 2007

Tumblr
www.tumblr.com
Launched in November 2007

the service in a short, concise way—and they make it really easy to do so. There may be extra bells and whistles with each of the services I have mentioned so far, but the purpose of a microblogging application is to allow people to express themselves in a way that can be read on the Web, through an IM client, through a desktop client, or on a cell phone. It is all about the social aspects of social networking!

Lifestreaming applications (also referred to as "social aggregators") are services that combine status updates (such as posts to Twitter, Plurk, or Identi.ca as well as to Facebook), information feeds, and other outputs of several different social sites into one interface. The most popular of these services, FriendFeed, allows you not only to see your social activities in one spot and with one interface but also to follow other people and see the updates to the services they are sharing on the aggregator's site. FriendFeed's innovation is that it allows a person to comment on anything that is shared via the FriendFeed service. Even if the original post does not allow direct commenting (such as a Twitter post), you can directly comment on it via FriendFeed. This comment can even be sent as a Twitter response if you have a Twitter account as well.

Aggregators, in general, are services that reduce the amount of time necessary to gather information. Feed readers—those applications that pull together many different blog feeds like Google Reader or Bloglines—are aggregators of RSS feeds. As a social aggregator, FriendFeed allows the users to collect all of their friends' social updates into one place and follow them easily—which reduces the amount of time required to follow each friend on each social site (such as Facebook, Twitter, Pownce, Plurk, any blog, Google Talk notifications, and much more). By aggregating all of this information together, FriendFeed can create a very detailed picture of a particular person's life. Because of this, some people who use FriendFeed make their lifestreams private so that anyone who wants to read what they are doing on each service has to be approved as a follower before accessing the information.

FriendFeed's great strength is the number of services that it will work with. Users can choose to share their updates from any of almost 40 different social sites—and from any blog or application that outputs an RSS feed that can be read in a feed reader. Users who choose to do so could dump all of the output of all of their social accounts into this one site and use it to create a river of information about their social networking life. They can make the information stream public and let anyone who is interested see everything they are posting on any site in the social networking sphere.

Because it is a "beta" service (beta just means that the service is ready for use but not necessarily in its final form, so it is still being tested and refined), FriendFeed is constantly adding new features to its offerings. One of the features added since the service launched that is proving to be popular is the ability to separate the people whose streams you follow into various category lists, so you can check just your professional contacts, your personal contacts, the people you think are funny, technologically plugged in, or just plain odd. This has become a big hit because of its ability to limit the amount of information and "noise" that comes at you as you are reading the combined lifestreams of all of the people you follow. Two other features that have been added since FriendFeed was first made public are (1) an IM notification service that has refined filters built in so that you do not get overwhelmed by the conversation and get only the posts you want and (2) the ability to post things on FriendFeed and have them also posted to Twitter. The second feature, the feed publishing service, lets you fine-tune what gets posted to Twitter and what doesn't, so you are not repeatedly putting the same posts on the Twitter service as you use both social sites.

FriendFeed is not the only lifestreaming application available, however—just the most popular. Tumblr—a "tumblelog" (or tumblog) application—is also a lifestreaming service. A tumblelog is a cross between a microblog and a lifestream. In a Tumblr blog, short, multimedia-rich posting is encouraged. Photos, videos, links, and quick thoughts are the general format of posts to Tumblr. People can subscribe to a particular Tumblr blog—just as they can with any other blog—but it does not really aggregate a number of people into a single interface like FriendFeed does.

Because of the short form of the Tumblr posts, they often consist of media clips (photos, videos, audio snippets, etc.) without much in the way of commentary from the creator. This allows people to follow the products of a particular person without the personal commentary that is common on longer format blogs. People do not expect more than a media post, link, or short quote from each post. This makes Tumblr interesting for busy people (or librarians) who just want to put their creative efforts out there without having to include a lot of text to go along with the post.

Tumblr provides a "widget"—a bit of code from a third-party Web site—that you embed into your own Web site to display content from that third-party site and to display your tumblog on another Web site. The editor of this series of books, Ellyssa Kroski, uses the Tumblr widget to add content into her Web site at www.ellyssakroski.com (see Figure 1.1). This gives her another way to add value to her main Web site and lets her easily post content to her tumblog that can be reused—a great time-saver when you have content that needs to be in multiple places. In the screenshot of her site (Figure 1.1), you can see that she is pulling information from both of her blogs as well as her Delicious, Facebook, and Flickr feeds. All of this is being run on the "backend" by Tumblr.

FriendFeed and Tumblr are the most popular sites in the aggregator/lifestreaming category and, as such, the most likely to have a significant number of your patrons with existing accounts. Other aggregation services include iStalkr (www.istalkr.com), Secondbrain (www.secondbrain.com), ProfileFly (http://profilefly.com), and

▶ Figure 1.1: Ellyssa Kroski's Web Site with Tumblr Widget (www.ellyssakroski.com)

Ellyssa**Kroski**
An emerging tech information consultant / librarian / writer / speaker / instructor

My Digital Stream

This is an aggregated feed of my blogs iLibrarian and InfoTangle, as well as my del.icio.us links, Flickr photos, and Facebook activity.

1. 10 Twitter Best Practices for Brands
   Michael Brito, social media strategist and community builder at Intel, blogs for Mashable about 10 Twitter Best Practices for Brands. The article discusses the art of using Twitter effectively for...
2. Duke University Libraries Image Collections for iPhone

About this Site

Welcome! This is the place to find out about my current and upcoming projects /available workshops / webcasts / talks /courses as well as to read the aggregated content from both of my blogs (iLibrarian and InfoTangle), my del.icio.us bookmarks, Flickr photos, and Facebook posted items.

Profilactic (www.profilactic.com). Other lifestreaming services include LifeStrea.ms (http://lifestrea.ms), Soup (www.soup.io), and Onaswarm (http://onaswarm.com).

▶ CHOOSING YOUR SERVICE

The choice of which particular service you use should depend entirely on which services your patrons use. Pay attention when you are out at your local coffee shop or Internet café and see what your community is using to communicate. Ask your patrons during any kind of survey or patron questionnaire what they use. Pick the service that is most in use by your community, and you will have a ready-made base of subscribers, or followers, who won't have to do more than click a button to become your library's friend on Twitter, Plurk, Tumblr, or FriendFeed. Once you have a few local followers, check out their lists of friends and see if they can "introduce" you to other locals whom you might not yet know. Use the search features to find folks who are in your zip code(s). Create accounts on all of these services, and use a service like ping.fm (www.ping.fm) to send out single messages to all of the different lifestreaming and microblogging services. Choose any one (or all) of these approaches to deciding which services you want to put your time and effort into using and maintaining.

▶2

PLANNING

- ▶ Define Uses for Microblogging/Lifestreaming in Your Library
- ▶ Get Administrative Buy-In
- ▶ Make It Work for You
- ▶ Ask Questions
- ▶ Create an Account

Before you jump into microblogging or aggregating your content, take some time to plan just what you want to do. There are many ways you can use a Twitter account alone, so figuring out how your library would want to make use of this tool will keep your account consistent. Keep in mind the many ways in which these services can be used, and prepare marketing materials, staff time, and other resources for the account in advance so that you are not caught by surprise when the account starts to get some use. Spend some time visiting other libraries (virtually, at least) that are using the services in the same way you plan to use them to get an idea of how they are handling their accounts. Use the services themselves to ask questions—Twitter is famous for the five-second response to questions that users send as a tweet, especially if the question is about Twitter itself. FriendFeed is also a good place to get answers to questions about how other libraries are using the service.

▶ DEFINE USES FOR MICROBLOGGING/ LIFESTREAMING IN YOUR LIBRARY

Some of the more common uses of a microblogging account involve patron notification:

- ▶ Communicate with patrons—send out messages in whatever way they would like to receive them: a desktop client, the Web, or IM or text messages on their phone.
- ▶ Engage patrons—if you have staff who are willing to be active users on the library's account, you can:
  - ➤ have conversations with your patrons,
  - ➤ answer their questions with resources at the library, and
  - ➤ remind them that you are there if they need you.
- ▶ Get feedback from patrons, seeking out comments and concerns about your services.
- ▶ Provide announcements for:
  - ➤ events,
  - ➤ news updates (i.e., library closings and other timely information),
  - ➤ new or interesting Web resource recommendations, and
  - ➤ new books.
- ▶ Write 140-character book reviews for your patrons!

Receiving comments from patrons requires some work to set up notifications every time your library's name comes up on one of the services. Once this is done, it is just a matter of letting your patrons know that you are there, listening and ready to take care of the issues that they have with the library.

Lifestreaming applications have their uses in a library as well:

- ▶ Gather together all of the "stuff" that the library puts out—RSS feeds from blogs, Twitter announcements and posts, Flickr pictures, etc.—and pull all of this information into one place for patrons.
- ▶ Use the stream as a way to highlight your library's resources and tools. For example:
  - ➤ put links to new services in your Delicious account and
  - ➤ aggregate all of the blogs from all of the libraries in your area.

▶ Join the local conversation—there are people in your service area who have FriendFeed accounts and who would think that being able to "talk" to their local library through a site that they enjoy is pretty cool.

Once you have identified your purposes for using microblogging and lifestreaming at your library, discuss them with your administrators and sell them on the idea of easy, free, and almost constant communication with your patron base. Of course, there is no reason to stick with just one account per service—accounts are free and the ability to segment off parts of your announcements to particular audiences (kids, adults, businesses, etc.) is powerful. Do not feel that you have to be limited to one account per service!

▶ GET ADMINISTRATIVE BUY-IN

Getting your administration to back a lifestreaming or microblogging initiative can be tricky. Because many administrators may not have heard of or used either Twitter or FriendFeed, start at the very beginning. Explain exactly what the services are, what they can do for your library, and how they can save your library money and time in the end. If your library is considering reaching out to patrons via text messaging, point out that Twitter is a good, free way to do this without using library bandwidth, server space, or any money from the budget. If your library is thinking about how to gather all of your communications to patrons in one place, explain that a FriendFeed account can do this and allow patrons to comment, as well.

If the library administration's objection to the social networking scene is that anyone can comment at any time about anything, use the examples in this book to point out the great benefits that many libraries are seeing while reporting very few problems. FriendFeed and Tumblr—the two major lifestreaming applications—both allow you to moderate the comments. If your administration refuses to allow your patrons to comment without some sort of filter, you can moderate the comments left on either platform easily.

▶ MAKE IT WORK FOR YOU

Once you have convinced your administration of the utility of these social networking services, you are ready to start planning how you are going to make the services work for your library. One way to do this is to learn how other libraries are using the various services. Some libraries, like the Casa Grande Public Library in Casa Grande, Arizona (www.twitter.com/cglibrary), use Twitter to highlight books in the catalog (with direct links to the material) as well as events that are coming up (see Figure 2.1). Most of their tweets are links to more information about books or events.

Other libraries, like the Missouri River Regional Library (MRRL) in Jefferson City, Missouri (www.twitter.com/mrrl), pull in blog posts, Flickr picture uploads, and event notices and include some "chatty" tweets as well, asking for responses from the community about a number of different topics (see Figure 2.2). Later in this chapter, when I discuss third-party applications for Twitter, I will explain just how all of these different feeds from blogs, Flickr, and other sources can be integrated into a Twitter feed to reduce the amount of staff time needed to update the service.

▶ Figure 2.1: Casa Grande Library's Twitter Homepage (www.twitter.com/cglibrary)

▶ Figure 2.2: MRRL's Twitter Stream from the Library's Homepage (www.mrrl.org)

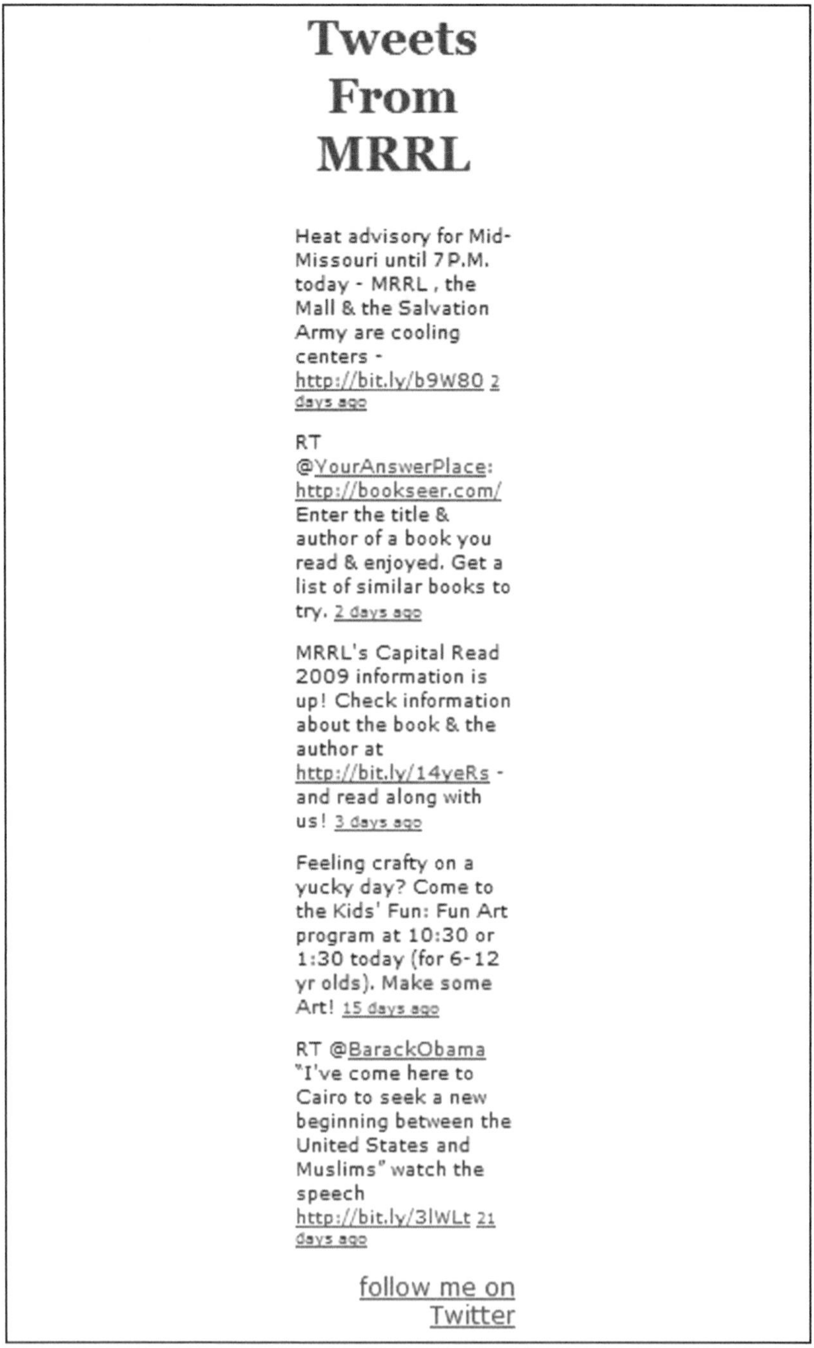

Tweets From MRRL

Heat advisory for Mid-Missouri until 7 P.M. today - MRRL , the Mall & the Salvation Army are cooling centers - http://bit.ly/b9W80 2 days ago

RT @YourAnswerPlace: http://bookseer.com/ Enter the title & author of a book you read & enjoyed. Get a list of similar books to try. 2 days ago

MRRL's Capital Read 2009 information is up! Check information about the book & the author at http://bit.ly/14yeRs - and read along with us! 3 days ago

Feeling crafty on a yucky day? Come to the Kids' Fun: Fun Art program at 10:30 or 1:30 today (for 6-12 yr olds). Make some Art! 15 days ago

RT @BarackObama "I've come here to Cairo to seek a new beginning between the United States and Muslims" watch the speech http://bit.ly/3lWLt 21 days ago

follow me on Twitter

Planning your use of FriendFeed, Tumblr, or another aggregation service can be easy. A major benefit of the services is to get all of your library's announcements and creative outputs (Flickr pictures, YouTube videos, blog content, etc.) and the conversations from these outputs into one spot for others to view or for you to reuse. For patrons, subscribing to a FriendFeed account from their local library, even if it does nothing more than display the library's events, pictures, videos, and blog posts, is a great way to stay informed about what is going on. For libraries, being able to take the RSS feed from the river of information that the organization puts out and reuse it by displaying it on the library's Web site, making it available to other organizations—the local Chamber of Commerce or the educational institution that the library supports, for example—is a time-saver. Just being aware of the conversation that is going on around the information you put out keeps you better in tune with your patrons' needs and wants. Any of these uses can make a FriendFeed or Tumblr account valuable enough to spend the time setting it up!

Some library-related organizations have FriendFeed accounts that are useful to libraries as well. The American Library Association's TechSource division has a FriendFeed account (http://friendfeed.com/alatechsource) that redisplays all the tweets and blog posts from the TechSource bloggers. This makes it convenient for libraries to follow the conversation that the TechSource folks begin in one spot and with a quick scan, rather than losing it in the quickly moving Twitter stream or having to keep the TechSource

Personal FriendFeed Accounts

There is a personal reason to use FriendFeed that may not directly involve your library at all and might not require much in the way of planning, either. FriendFeed is an excellent way to join the conversation—even as a single librarian—and make your voice known and your opinions heard in the larger conversation about libraries. Even if your library as an organization decides not to use FriendFeed, you can use it with a personal account to keep up with trends, events, and thoughts that are circulating through the library world.

Twitter and blog pages open all the time. Because this is FriendFeed, libraries can get involved in the conversation as well by commenting on items posted. This is what your library can do for your patrons—give them a single source of information about your events, activities, and news, with the ability to create a conversation at the same time.

▶ ASK QUESTIONS

Before you create your Twitter, FriendFeed, or Tumblr accounts, ask yourself, and answer, these questions:

▶ What will change as a result of this account? Do you see anything being different in a few months? What?

▶ Who do you hope to connect with using Twitter, FriendFeed, or Tumblr? What kind of information will they find useful and interesting? What will people expect of this account?

▶ What can go wrong with the account? What plans are in place for "too much" popularity, friends or followers who are abusive, etc.?

Consider OpenMicroBlogging

One thing to plan for before you create an account at one of these services is what you are going to do if the service fails. Twitter is notoriously unstable, and there are countless articles on the Internet that talk about the pain that people feel when the Twitter service is disrupted. One way to help mitigate the risk of your chosen service becoming unavailable is to support the OpenMicroBlogging standard.

According to its Web site, OpenMicroBlogging is an "effort to create an open standard for microblogging . . . a specification that allows different messaging hubs to route microblogging messages between users in a near-realtime timeframe" (http://openmicro blogging.org/about). This effort would take the load off of individual services like Twitter and allow all microblogging services to use the same infrastructure and share the load. This is, however, somewhat like the chat "wars" of a few years ago, when AOL and other chat providers refused to open their chat protocols in an effort to keep people locked into their service. Today, you can download an IM client such as Trillian (www.ceruleanstudios.com) and connect to multiple chat servers through the same software and using the same protocols. Microblogging may follow this path in opening standards and allowing users of Twitter to send messages to users of Plurk or Identi.ca. For now, however, the standards used by each service are different. In the case of Plurk and Twitter, the standards are closed. Identi.ca is one of the services that supports OpenMicroBlogging natively. Until the services hash out how to manage an open standard and how to stay competitive, you will have to decide if going with an open standard such as Identi.ca is worth losing the people who are already using Twitter.

▶ CREATE AN ACCOUNT

As with all social networking services, you must have an account to begin using Twitter, FriendFeed, Tumblr, or any of the other applications mentioned. For the most part, getting an account is easy and quick—there are usually no more than three to five informational text boxes to fill out. Once you've filled them in and decided whether or not you want your account to be private—viewable only by people you approve to follow you—or public—viewable by anyone with an account at that service— you are ready to start finding friends and using the service.

A discussion of privacy settings is in order before we start. Each of the major services offers a "private" feed setting that allows only those who you have approved to follow your updates on the service to see your posts or your stream from a lifestreaming application. Because this book is written for libraries, and libraries are generally open and available to the public, it makes sense for us to make our accounts public as well. Creating a private feed will limit the number of people who choose to follow you—many people want to see what kinds of things you post before they commit to pressing that "follow" or "subscribe" button—and it will limit how easily others can use your updates and information.

Twitter

Twitter is, at heart, a text messaging service. If you want to do any Web-based administering of your content, however, you would have to visit the Web site and sign up. While administration of accounts via the text messaging service for Twitter is increasingly possible, most people choose to use the Web site to do most of their administrative activities, such as following other people or updating their status. The Twitter homepage, for example, includes a large, obvious button to press to sign up (see Figure 2.3).

Once you have pressed the button labeled "Sign Up Now" on the Twitter homepage, you get a very short form to fill out to create your account. All it asks for is your username, password, and e-mail

CAPTCHA

The CAPTCHA (Completely Automated Public Turing test to tell Computers and Humans Apart) system (http://en.wikipedia .org/wiki/Captcha) is intended to weed out automated "bots" (computer programs that spammers use to sign up for accounts, place comments on blogs, and create opportunities for themselves to spam others on the service) that attempt to create accounts on social networks so that they can friend and then spam other users. The CAPTCHA field in a form presents some sort of text-based image that computers cannot easily read, on the theory that a real human being could read it and type in the text shown in the image. Some sites, including Twitter, use a service called reCAPTCHA (http://recaptcha.net/) that solves at least one of the major complaints about CAPTCHAs—the fact that they are not accessible to blind users. The reCAPTCHA service that Twitter uses also includes a spoken test that blind users can play and then type in the words that they hear. reCAPTCHA does double duty by both protecting a site from spammers and helping digitize books by presenting text that the computer cannot read as the CAPTCHA and allowing the humans signing up for the service to decipher the text for the digitization project.

▶ Figure 2.3: Twitter Sign-Up Screen #1

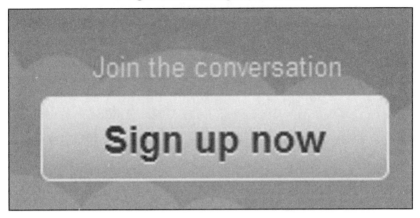

address. It also uses a "CAPTCHA" spam-fighting system that asks you to type in the words that you see in the box. This makes it difficult for automated systems to sign up for multiple accounts to spam the system. You can then sign up for the e-mail updates, if you like, or read the Terms of Service for Twitter from that screen. Once you have entered your information, click on the "Create My Account" button as shown in Figure 2.4, and you are done. This is all that is required to sign up for a Twitter account.

Now that you have your account, you can log in via the Web site and answer that question about what you are doing now. When you log into your account on Twitter, you will first see your "tweet stream," consisting of all of your friends' tweets. If you have not made any friends yet, the screen will be blank. If you click on the "Home" link at the top right of the page, you will see the text box that asks the question,

Followers vs. Friends

Followers, in Twitter, are people who receive your status updates to the Twitter service. Friends are people whose status updates you receive. These two groups are not mutually exclusive; you can have followers who are also friends. They do not, however, have to be the same, either. You can have friends (people you follow) who are not following you (they are not one of your followers) and vice versa.

▶ Figure 2.4: Twitter Sign-Up Screen #2

Already use Twitter on your phone? Finish signup now.

Full name

Username

Your URL: http://twitter.com/USERNAME

Password

Email

☐ I want the inside scoop—please send me email updates!

uɒɑ   **iota**

Can't read this?
↻ Get two new words
◀ Listen to the words
Powered by reCAPTCHA
Help

Type the words above

Create my account

"what are you doing now?" Take a moment to answer it—even if you have no friends yet, you can see what your tweets look like in your Twitter stream.

Twitter's Options

From your Twitter homepage on the Web, you can view your profile, find people (much more about this later), adjust your settings, and get help. All of these options are found at the top right of the page. Your profile consists of a picture, a link, and a brief biography of you or your organization. After this information, the number of people you follow and who follow you and the number of updates you have made to Twitter (the number of posts you have sent out) are shown. The main part of the page, the left column, is what you have posted to Twitter—it is just your tweets alone, so you can review them easily and remind yourself of what you have been posting.

Twitter's Homepage

The service's homepage itself gives a good deal of information. There you will find the text box you can use to post, along with a reminder of your last post to the service located just under that.

You also get another view of your statistics—how many follow you, how many you follow, how many posts you have sent out—and then you have links along the right side to even more features of the Twitter system:

@username: Twitter allows directed conversations to occur by the "@" or "at" reply system. Direct messages—a private method of communication—can be read by only the person being messaged. If you want to ask a specific person a question without everyone seeing it, this is the way to do it.

Favorites: A way to keep tweets that you enjoy or want to save.

Everyone timeline: Includes the posts from every Twitter user whose account is not set to private. When something big is going on in the world, reading the Everyone timeline is a great way to keep up with the latest developments.

Images of followers: A block of images of people who are following your Twitter stream. Below the block of people is the option to quickly turn phone or IM notifications on or off.

Other areas linked from the Twitter homepage include:

Profile page: A page with just your tweets. Also, there is a link to the tweets you have marked as your favorites (which you can mark by clicking the star icon next to the particular tweet that you want to save) and the numbers of all of the people who are following your Twitter account.

Conversational Twitter

Twitter uses the @reply syntax to create directed conversations. If you want a tweet to reply directly to another Twitter user, you put the @ symbol before their Twitter username and they will be alerted to the post through the "mentions" area of the Twitter site, or through their desktop client, whichever they use. When you ask a question, the @reply system gives you an easy way to collect answers as well, as folks who answer it will use the @yourusername convention to make sure you see their responses.

Settings page: Gives you tools to change your name, e-mail address, the link that you choose to use for your profile, your "one line bio" that you can write describing yourself or your organization, and your location. This area is also where you can set your account to be protected—or private—so that only people you approve can see your posts.

Texting with Twitter

Phone notification is part of what makes Twitter so handy, but it can also be very distracting and possibly expensive if you do not have an unlimited text messaging plan. Being able to turn the notifications off when you need to work distraction-free, either from text messaging or from IM, can be very helpful.

Reusable RSS

On just about every page of the Twitter Web site is a link to get the RSS feed for that page. This means that not only can you read your Twitter stream on the Web site, in your IM client, and via your phone, but you can also add your Twitter stream to your feed reader to read it there as well. You can do much more with an RSS feed, too—it is a standard XML language that can be reused in many different ways.

One of the most common ways to reuse a feed is to display it on an unrelated Web page as a news box or list of headlines. You can also use a service such as Yahoo! Pipes (http://pipes.yahoo.com) to combine feeds and output them in XML, RSS, or HTML for use on Web pages as more than just a list of headlines. Pipes gives you the ability to filter for keywords in a feed, to remove duplicates from multiple feeds, and to include user input to customize which parts of a feed or feeds are shown. Beyond that, since the RSS feed is XML, it can be used as input to a large number of Web mashups, including mapping locations mentioned in a Twitter stream, using the keywords from a FriendFeed stream in an Amazon.com search query to find books that pertain to the discussion, and much, much more.

Twitter's Application Programming Interface

An application programming interface (API) is a set of programming "hooks" that allow developers to use the features of a particular application, such as Twitter, in their own Web sites and applications. Twitter has a very good API with lots of ways to interact with the service in order to make it work for you. Check out the Recommended Resources in the last chapter of the book to find some pointers to ways you can use the API to interact with Twitter from your own Web pages or applications.

FriendFeed

When you go to the FriendFeed Web site at www.friendfeed.com (see Figure 2.5), you will see a large button that invites you to "Join FriendFeed." This link leads you to the FriendFeed sign-up form, which has just five text fields to fill in. Enter in your e-mail address, real name, the nickname that you want displayed to the FriendFeed community (you can change this later, very easily), and then your chosen password, twice. On this page, you choose your level of privacy—"public" means that anyone with an account can read your posts, and "private" means that only people you allow are able to read what you post to FriendFeed. There is also a link to both the Terms of Use and the Privacy Policy for FriendFeed on this page. Be sure to look over this information to make sure you are comfortable with the level of security and privacy that FriendFeed offers.

▶ Figure 2.5: FriendFeed Sign-Up Screen #1

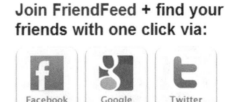

Click the "Create my account »" button (see Figure 2.6) and you are done—you have a FriendFeed account! From there, it is just a matter of finding friends and joining the conversation to get a basic level of benefit from the system. Of course, there is much more that you can do to tweak your FriendFeed experience.

This is only one way to get a FriendFeed account, however. FriendFeed also lets you create an account using your Facebook, Google, or Twitter account credentials. This means that if you create your Twitter account, then go to FriendFeed and click on the "Twitter" button to create your account using your Twitter log-in credentials, you only have to remember one set of credentials to get into both accounts. If you have cookies turned on in your browser, you can also log into one account and then go to the other service and already be logged into it without having to reenter your information.

Import Services

The first thing to do once you get your account set up is to add some services to FriendFeed so that you have some content coming in. There is a link to "Import Site" on your FriendFeed

▶ Figure 2.6: FriendFeed Sign-Up Screen #2

homepage; click on that to see the list of 50+ services (available at the time of this writing; see Figure 2.7) that you can import to your FriendFeed account. Go through the list and find the services that you currently use. If you have a blog, you can enter the blog's RSS feed address under the "Blogging" heading. You can do the same

▶ Figure 2.7: FriendFeed Import Services

Blogging
🐾 Ameba
🔲 Blog
🖊 LiveJournal
🔲 Skyrock
🆃 Tumblr
🈲 百度空间

Bookmarking
▪️ delicious
🔗 Diigo
🅵 Furl
❀ Ma.gnolia
🔲 Mister Wong
🔲 StumbleUpon
🔲 Twine
🔲 はてな

Books
g Goodreads
🅛 LibraryThing

News
🔲 Digg
🔲 Google Reader
🔲 menéame
🔲 Mixx
🔲 Reddit

Photos
•• Flickr
🔲 Fotolog
🔲 Photobucket
🔲 Picasa Web Albums
🔲 SmugMug
🆉 Zooomr

Status
🅑 brightkite.com
🅕 Facebook
🔲 Gmail/Google Talk
🆀 identi.ca
🅿 Plurk
🔲 Twitter

Music
🔲 iLike
🔲 Last.fm
🅿 Pandora

Comments
🅑 Backtype
🅓 Disqus
🔲 Intense Debate

Video
12 12seconds
🔲 Dailymotion
🅹 Joost
🔲 Seesmic
🔲 Smotri.com
🆅 Vimeo
🔲 YouTube

Miscellaneous
🔲 Custom RSS/Atom
🔲 Amazon.com
🔲 LinkedIn
🔲 Netflix
🔲 Netvibes
🔲 Polyvore
🔲 SlideShare
⭐ tipjoy
🔲 Upcoming
∞ Wakoopa
🔲 Yelp

for each of the other services—there are specific instructions for each service about how to add that service to your account. Once you have entered the feeds and status update URLs from each service you use (and don't forget that the Twitter posts you make are also status updates), you can then see a list of "My Services" at the right side of the box. This list lets you know what services you are importing and gives you the opportunity to make changes to the service or to stop importing it whenever you like.

Other links from the top of the page, near the Import Site link, are for adding messages, links and photos directly to your FriendFeed lifestream. They can be found after the word "Post:" at the top of your FriendFeed homepage.

FriendFeed's Features

FriendFeed's utility links are at the top right of your FriendFeed home page. They start with a link labeled with your FriendFeed name. Clicking on that link gets you a page with nothing but your contributions to FriendFeed. Listed there are messages you have posted, status updates from other sites that you have imported, and comments that you have made to other people's FriendFeed content.

These are the rest of the utility links:

- ▶ "Friends" gives you a number of different ways to view the list of friends you have on the FriendFeed service.
- ▶ "Tools" link takes you to a page full of ways to post to FriendFeed easily, share your feed with others, and access your feed many different ways.
- ▶ "Account" goes to a page that lets you change:
  - ➤ your feed preferences, including:
    - your display name,
    - your nickname,
    - the language in which you are posting,
    - your password, and
    - another way to edit or add to the services that you import into FriendFeed;

> ➤ the level of privacy for your feed;
> ➤ the method you want FriendFeed to use to contact you when someone subscribes to you, comments on a post of yours, or just whether you want a daily e-mail with a summary of you and your friends' activities on the site; and
> ➤ fine-grained decisions about what kinds of things get posted and how your published feed is composed.

Once you have started to use your FriendFeed account, you will be able to comment on other user's posts or "like" those posts. Commenting is straightforward—you click the "Comment" link that is below each post and type in your response. Liking a post is also easy—you click the word "Like" below the post to indicate that you approve of the post or enjoy it in some way. Some people only like posts, and others like the post and then comment on it. Still others only comment and never like any posts at all. How you use your account is up to you, but FriendFeed gives you many ways to interact with the other people using the service.

Another security feature that FriendFeed offers is the Remote Key. To find your Remote Key, go to http://friendfeed.com/account/api. This key gives other applications a way to access your FriendFeed account, including posting things in your name, without having to give up your FriendFeed password. Some of the third-party applications that will be discussed later in this book use the Remote Key to work with FriendFeed.

Lists in FriendFeed

FriendFeed also includes two very handy tools that make FriendFeed much more usable than it was when it was initially released. First is the ability to create lists of friends that you can view separately. This really cuts down on the speed of updates in FriendFeed's real-time stream, and it can help make your FriendFeed friends easier to follow. You can put friends in your home list (the default, standard list that everyone uses), or you can create as many lists as you need to separate out friends from your job, your home, or your social set. For libraries, this means that you can still follow other libraries, but you can separate those accounts out from the local patrons to whom you may want to pay closer attention.

Rooms in FriendFeed

The other handy tool is the Rooms feature. FriendFeed allows anyone to create a room, either private or public, and anyone can join any public room. For libraries, this means you can create your own room to discuss local issues and invite local users of FriendFeed to participate. There is much more, however, that you can do with your FriendFeed account—I will be covering most of what you can do with an account later in the book.

Tumblr

Tumblr, another lifestreaming service that aggregates much of your online activity, makes it just as easy to create an account. Go to the site at www.tumblr.com; enter your e-mail address, password, and Tumblr URL—the address where your posts will be found; and click on the "Start Posting" button. This can be accessed directly from the homepage of the site, as shown in Figure 2.8.

If you chose to use the 10-second sign-up link, you will see a form, exactly like the one on the homepage, asking for your e-mail address, your password, and the URL that you would like to use for your tumblelog. Click the "Sign up and start posting!" button (see Figure 2.9), and you will be ready to begin aggregating your online presence in one, easy-to-point-to place.

Start Posting in Tumblr

Once you have logged in, you will immediately see the Tumblr dashboard. The first thing they ask you to do is to post something—you can easily post video, audio, images, text, or links as well as a specially formatted "quote" posting form. Once you have posted something and checked out your new page, you can go to the "Account" link to make changes to your e-mail address, your password, the editor you prefer to use, and the look of your account's dashboard.

▶ Figure 2.8: Tumblr Sign-Up Screen

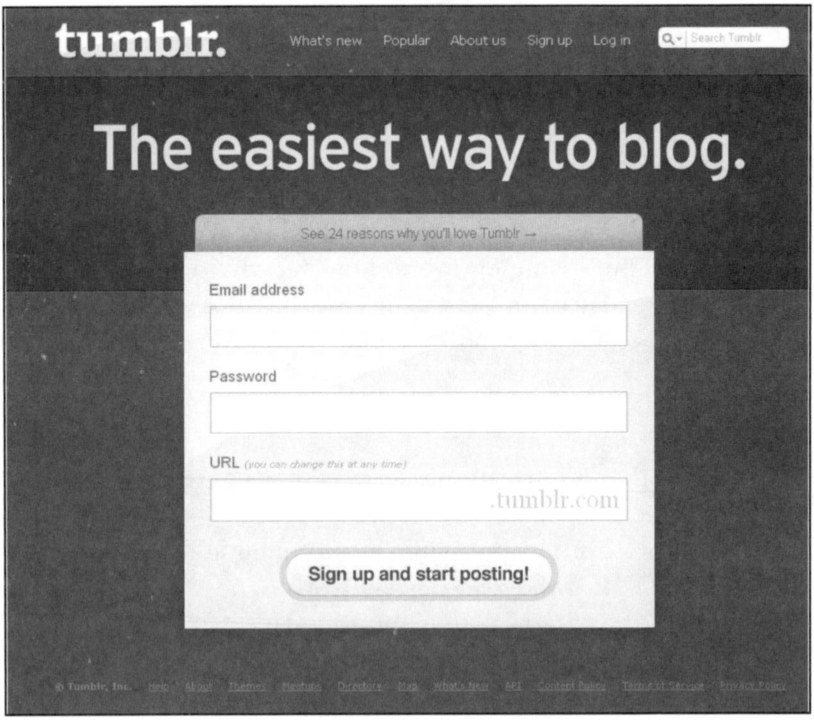

▶ Figure 2.9: Tumblr Sign-Up Form

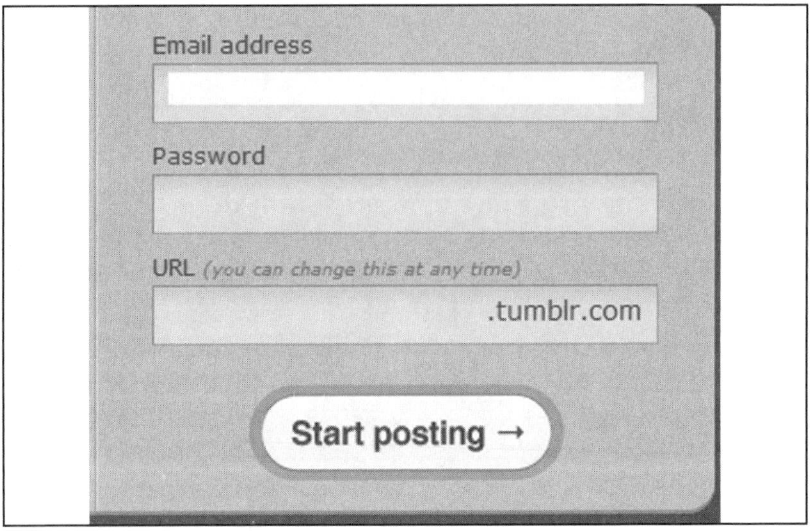

Customize Tumblr

From the "Account" page, there is a link to the Customize feature of Tumblr. This page gives you the ability to change your site's information—the title, description, photo, and URL of your Tumblr blog—as well as the theme and appearance of the site. On this page as well is the way to add feeds to your Tumblr blog. This is what makes Tumblr into a lifestreaming service. Unlike FriendFeed, however, you can add up to only five other sites, so you must choose what you are importing carefully. Finally, the "Advanced" tab on the page gives you lots of options. You have the ability to set your time zone, add custom CSS coding to your Tumblr blog, decide what options you would like to enable for your blog, including how to handle links—if they should open in a new window or not—and whether or not to use descriptive URLs for your Tumblr blog links.

Others in Use

The lifestreaming/microblogging landscape changes frequently. The success of Twitter and FriendFeed ensured that there would be people who would take the basic idea and attempt to improve it or add to it. Many of them have already gone away. Others are still around—and still in use—but are not used nearly as much as the "big three" services of Twitter, FriendFeed, and Tumblr.

Another category of microblogging services is the enterprise service. Yammer, introduced in Chapter 1, is a good example of this kind of software. Because it has a very limited reach, and because it is not where your library patrons will be, I will not be talking about this or any other secure, enterprise-level service. It is available, however, if you would like to create a library in-house Twitter-like communication service that does not involve your patrons.

One "other" service I would like to discuss briefly is the self-hosted, open source microblogging platform StatusNet (www .status.net; formerly known as Laconi.ca). This software runs the Twitter competitor Identi.ca and is freely available for anyone who wants to run his or her own microblogging system. This can be used as either a completely internal messaging system, similar to

Yammer, but even more closed and secure because it can live entirely behind an organization's firewall and does not require access to the open Internet to work, or a more-stable replacement for Twitter, something that your organization can use in much the same ways people use Twitter but without the dangers of server overloads and DDOS attacks.

DDOS Attacks

DDOS (Distributed Denial of Service) Attacks are particularly effective against free and open communication services such as Twitter, Facebook, and Tumblr. The DDOS attack involves many different "zombie" computers—computers that have been compromised and taken over by hackers—that flood a Web site or service with so many requests that the service collapses under the load, becoming impossible for anyone to use.

In August 2009, there was a large DDOS attack (as explained in an article in PCWorld magazine, available at: www.pcworld.com/businesscenter/article/169893/ddos_attackers_continue_hitting_twitter_facebook_google.html) that crippled Twitter for a day and made it less than reliable for almost a week. A self-hosted microblog could help avoid this kind of service outage.

StatusNet has a thriving development community around it and looks to be a stable platform to use—although you must take into account the fact that it is not the "industry leader" and, as such, does not have the name recognition that a Twitter account would have. Because Twitter is still mostly an early-adopter service—the majority of Internet users are not using it—you have the time to decide which platform your organization wants to use and the opportunity to take your patrons or staff members with you. As Twitter's popularity and use grows, however, without the advent of something like the OpenMicroBlogging standard (discussed at the beginning of this chapter), each of these microblogging services will be stand-alone applications that you must post to individually (if you use both) unless you can make a case for people to create yet another account.

▶3

IMPLEMENTATION

- ▶ Feed Your Blog Posts into Twitter
- ▶ Feed Your Tweets into Your Web Site
- ▶ Use Twitter for Library News, Events, and Service Announcements
- ▶ Use Twitter and FriendFeed during Your Library Events
- ▶ Learn to Use the Search Features
- ▶ Download Helper Applications
- ▶ Build an Online Community

Now that you have an account (or two) at Twitter, FriendFeed, or Tumblr and some idea of how you will use them, the question is—what next? Understanding each of the services' strengths, and weaknesses, is crucial for effective use of the service. Make sure you spend some time using Twitter, FriendFeed, or Tumblr before you start publicizing the account. You want to be sure that you understand the conventions of the application and the culture of the participants before you jump in and make a mistake.

You can begin by adding RSS feeds to FriendFeed or Tumblr and posting tweets to Twitter, but using each service effectively—with minimal time and effort from staff—can be tricky. There are ways to automate Twitter so that it gets automatic content that other parts of your organization originally create, and there are ways to make FriendFeed and Tumblr less of a content graveyard and more of a conversation. Pick just a couple of the suggestions to follow in this chapter and try them. If they work at both reducing your workload and improving your library's communication with patrons, pick a couple more and try those, too!

▶ FEED YOUR BLOG POSTS INTO TWITTER

One of the easiest ways to start getting content into a Twitter account is to set up a blog feed to dump into your account automatically. You don't have to use a blog. Any application that can give information in RSS format—many online calendars or other social networking sites like Facebook—can be used as seed content for a fledgling Twitter account. All you have to do is find the RSS feed. Look for the standard RSS feed icon, shown in Figure 3.1, to find RSS feeds for most sites. Once you've got the address for the RSS feed, you can then use a third-party service to get all posts from that feed automatically added to your organization's Twitter stream.

Twitterfeed

Twitterfeed (www.twitterfeed.com) is a free service that takes an RSS feed address and monitors it for new posts. As soon as a post is published, Twitterfeed then uses your Twitter log-in credentials to post the title and a link to the post for you. What makes this kind of service so useful is the fact that you spend five or ten minutes setting it up once and then never think about it again—it continues to post for you as long as there are items being added to the RSS feed. The downside, however, is that the service is free, so there is no guarantee that it will be around tomorrow. If the Web site folds

▶ Figure 3.1: Standard RSS Feed Icon, in Use Around the Web

and stops providing the service, you are back to manually adding posts to Twitter until you can find a replacement.

Pingvine

Another service that does much the same thing as Twitterfeed is Pingvine (www.pingvine.com). What Pingvine does in addition, though, is send an RSS feed to Twitter and/or Identi.ca as well as to a social notification service called Ping.fm (www.ping.fm). This means that if you choose to use Identi.ca instead of Twitter, you have an alternative to the Twitter-only Twitterfeed. It also means that if you set up Ping.fm to alert your various social networks each time you update your status, your blog posts will automatically go out to all of the social networks you have set up through Ping.fm.

Social Notification Tools

Tools like Ping.fm help busy people keep all of their various social networking sites updated simultaneously. The concept is that you post an update once, and it is then sent out to any of the social sites that you have chosen to notify when setting up the account. HelloTxt (www.hellotxt.com) is another service that does the same thing—posts instant notification updates to Facebook, Twitter, FriendFeed, and many other sites with just one click.

▶ FEED YOUR TWEETS INTO YOUR WEB SITE

Keeping a Web site up-to-date and constantly fresh is a time-consuming job. The more you can automate adding content to your site, the easier it will be to maintain it and to keep people coming back to it. One way to add content to your site is to embed your Twitter stream into your Web site. This will ensure that your content changes regularly (as long as you are updating your Twitter statuses regularly, of course) and will give your Twitter account some added visibility to people who may be interested in following your library's tweets. Embedding your tweet stream into your Web site also makes your status updates reusable—you can write once (to Twitter) and have that information repurposed as fresh content for your Web site.

The easiest way to get your Tweets into your Web site is to use the Twitter badge or widget that Twitter makes available to all of its users. You can get one that displays all of your tweets at twitter.com/goodies/widgets. To create the widget, you first choose what type of site you will be installing the widget on—whether it is on your Web site, a Facebook page, or a MySpace page. If you choose Facebook or MySpace, you will get code for a Facebook application or MySpace widget that you can add to your profile pages on those services. If you choose to get code that you can insert into a Web site, you can then choose between a Profile widget (see Figure 3.2), a Search widget, a Faves widget, or a List widget. The Profile widget displays your tweets, the Search widget displays all of the results from a particular search and is good for keeping track of a topic on a blog or Web site devoted to that topic, the Faves widget displays all of the tweets that you have marked as your favorites, and the List widget displays all of the posts from everyone you have added to a particular list. All four widgets are provided as JavaScript code that you can insert anywhere in your Web page that you would like the widget to appear. The next screens ask you to customize your widget—preferences, appearance, and dimensions—and then you get the code that you need to insert into your Web site to make your tweets a part of your site.

Because Twitter provides RSS feeds and an API (application programming interface), there is no need to be limited to the widgets that they provide. You can use an RSS feed from your account (see Figure 3.3), or you can dig into the API documentation at http://apiwiki.twitter.com to see what other things you can do with your Twitter account for your library. One thing that will make working with an RSS feed easier is a service like Yahoo! Pipes (www.yahoo.com/pipes). This application takes RSS feeds and manipulates them—sorting, filtering, removing duplicates, and/ or combining in many different ways—and then creates another RSS feed with the manipulated content for you to use. For example, Missouri River Regional Library (MRRL), Jefferson City, takes its Twitter feed, runs it through Yahoo! Pipes, and removes any

▶ Figure 3.2: Missouri River Regional Library's Twitter Account Using the Flash Badge

Note: Requires Flash 9

tweets that do not contain the words "Bookmobile route." They then use this feed to populate their announcements area on their bookmobile Web page. This would work with multiple accounts, too. For this scenario, you could take all of your various Twitter accounts, combine them using Yahoo! Pipes, filter out the duplicate entries, and present them on your homepage using the RSS feed from Yahoo!.

▶ Figure 3.3: Missouri River Regional Library's Twitter Account Using RSS to Display on the Homepage

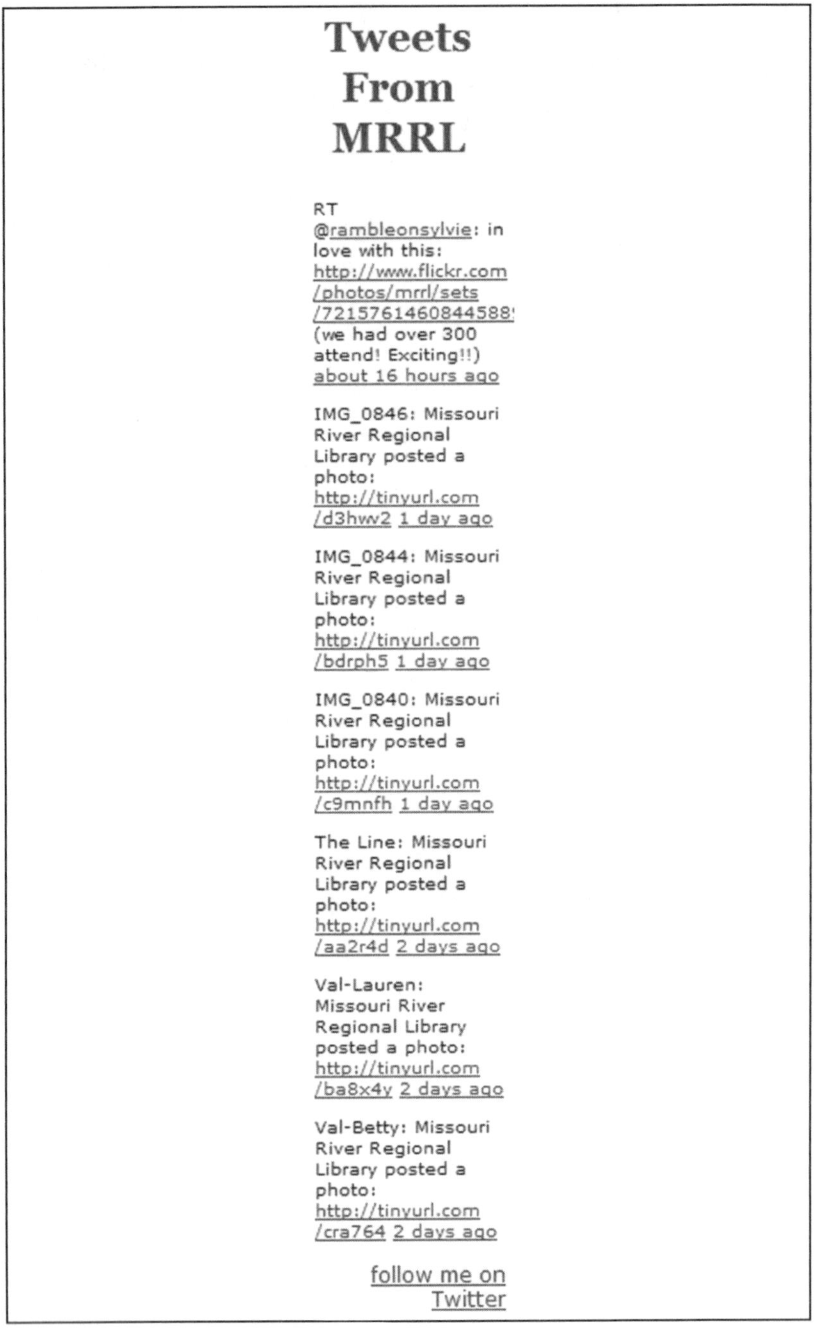

Tweets From MRRL

RT
@rambleonsylvie: in love with this:
http://www.flickr.com /photos/mrrl/sets /7215761460844588'
(we had over 300 attend! Exciting!!)
about 16 hours ago

IMG_0846: Missouri River Regional Library posted a photo:
http://tinyurl.com /d3hvv2 1 day ago

IMG_0844: Missouri River Regional Library posted a photo:
http://tinyurl.com /bdrph5 1 day ago

IMG_0840: Missouri River Regional Library posted a photo:
http://tinyurl.com /c9mnfh 1 day ago

The Line: Missouri River Regional Library posted a photo:
http://tinyurl.com /aa2r4d 2 days ago

Val-Lauren: Missouri River Regional Library posted a photo:
http://tinyurl.com /ba8x4y 2 days ago

Val-Betty: Missouri River Regional Library posted a photo:
http://tinyurl.com /cra764 2 days ago

follow me on Twitter

Further discussion of both using Yahoo! Pipes and adding RSS feeds to your library's Web pages is beyond the scope of this book, but there are helpful references and tutorials listed in the Web Resources section of the Recommended Resources chapter. Many of the tutorials are perfectly suitable for beginners—they require no more tech savvy than cutting and pasting a URL into a box. Some of the resources are wizards that will guide you through every step needed to take an RSS feed and display it on your Web page! Others are more advanced and will show you how to do very cool things with the information in your Twitter RSS feed. All of the RSS tutorials will also work with the RSS output of your FriendFeed or Tumblr account, too.

Tweets-to-Web Tools

Blog–Twitter Tools: Integrates your Twitter account with a Wordpress blog; allows you to tweet when you have a new post and to create a regular posting of all of your tweets for the day, week, or month (http://wordpress.org/extend/plugins/twitter-tools/).

RSS Feed: The raw XML information from your Twitter feed that can be used with Yahoo! Pipes or a JavaScript or Web scripting library (such as PHP's MagPie RSS parsing library) to display fully customizable views of your Twitter account (RSS feed found on your profile page near the bottom of the sidebar; MagPie at http://magpierss.sourceforge.net/).

Widgets–Twitter's widgets: Flash-based badges that require just a bit of code copy-and-paste to start displaying your tweets, custom search results, your favorite tweets, or all of the tweets from one of your lists (http://twitter.com/goodies/widgets).

Yahoo! Pipes: Drag-and-drop creation of custom feeds; allows you to enter several feeds (good for libraries with several tweeters who want to combine those tweets into a single information stream) and manipulate them—remove duplicates, filter for particular topics, etc. Results can be accessed as a badge to post on your Web site, Yahoo! or Google gadgets, in raw RSS or PHP formats, sent to an e-mail address, or added to a newsreader. Google, Netvibes, Bloglines, and Newsgator are supported as of this writing.

▶ USE TWITTER FOR LIBRARY NEWS, EVENTS, AND SERVICE ANNOUNCEMENTS

Because of the nature of Twitter—short, informative bursts of text that are broadcast to a group of people—you can easily use Twitter to inform your patrons about what your organization is doing. The chances are, however, that you are already doing this in another way. If you are using a blog, or a calendar of events that can produce RSS feeds, or posting news and service announcements to a social network of just about any type, you have an opportunity to reuse that information in your Twitter account. This will reduce the amount of original work that you must do to create announcement, event information, and service posts. If you are already doing it in one spot, you can reuse that information in Twitter.

For news announcements, if you already have a blog, you have an RSS feed that can be used to populate your Twitter account. Because Twitter is so mobile phone oriented, your patrons can choose to follow your Twitter account instead of your blog and get your announcements directly to their mobile phones. The mechanics of making this happen are laid out for you in a previous section of this book, "Feed Your Blog Posts into Twitter." For libraries that are part of a larger organization, such as a university or public library, there is an opportunity to get a feed from the parent organization's blog to use to inform your patrons of all of the news of the library and the larger organization. For public libraries, this could be the local chamber of commerce, city government office, or county government—any organization that produces news in an RSS format that you can then use to add value to your Twitter stream may be included.

Events, if entered into a calendaring application (such as Google's Calendar at www.google.com/calendar) that provides an RSS feed, are natural fits for a tweet letting people know what is going on. Even calendars that do not natively provide feeds are usable if they support the iCal standard or originate in Microsoft's Outlook program. iCal is an event description standard that many different calendars can use. If you can export the calendar to iCal format and import it into Google Calendar, you can still take advantage of Google's RSS feeds to add value to your Twitter stream.

Simply add a new calendar to an existing Google account—make sure you select import calendar when adding it—and then browse for your iCal event file or Outlook CSV file and import it. This is a manual process, but it is easier than retyping the events, and once the events are in Google, they are available for reuse in many different ways, including as entries in your Twitter stream.

Service announcements, such as MRRL's bookmobile route cancellations, are a natural fit for Twitter as well. Again, because Twitter is so easy to use with a mobile phone, people can get timely announcements about bookmobile issues, weather closings, or other changes in your services. You can do this manually or out-source the work to the decision makers using a service called TwitterMail (www.twittermail.com) to let the folks who decide when the route will be cancelled or when the library will be closed send out the announcement to Twitter via e-mail.

▶ USE TWITTER AND FRIENDFEED DURING YOUR LIBRARY EVENTS

Twitter and FriendFeed can be useful to promote, provide context for, and sustain library events and programs. They provide both a method of marketing that is free and effective and a way to keep the conversation going long after the last participants in your event have gone home. Adding information, links, and other "background" material to a Twitter stream or FriendFeed group will provide a base for discussion both during and after the program has finished. You can also use Twitter during the event to post real-time status reports on what is going on at that moment. This will provide motivation for people to show up and may give people who did not attend this time a bit more of a reason to do so next time!

Set Up a Group in Twitter/FriendFeed

Twitter has no built-in group function, but it does have a way to keep people together and to let everyone follow a conversation about your event or program. The hashtag, a word that is preceded by a pound sign (#), is Twitter's answer to a true grouping func-tion. Many people already use hashtags—they are very popular for keeping tweets about a particular conference together (and were used very effectively at the 2009 ALA midwinter conference) or for sustaining a conversation throughout a period of time. At the beginning of 2009, in early March, a spontaneous group event used the hashtag #queryfail. Editors and agents posted mistakes and problems in queries for articles and books that they had received. This proved to be very popular, giving writers a way to see what common mistakes were being made—so that they could avoid them—and letting editors and agents share stories, at 140 characters or less, of crazy queries that they had received. Because of the search tools that Twitter offers, people who didn't follow a bunch of editors or agents could still follow the conversation by searching for that particular hashtag.

Hashtags and Trends

Keeping up with hashtags can be done pretty easily just by going to the Twitter search page at http://search.twitter.com and checking out the "Trending Topics" listed on the page. The most popular hashtags in use—in real time—are listed just below the search text box on the search page.

You can also find the Trending Topics list on the search results page in a sidebar on the right side of the screen. In either place, you can click on any of the Trending Topics and Twitter will perform a search on that hashtag to give you a real-time view of the conversation as it happens. Either way you access the Trending Topics, you can find out what people are talking about right now and see what topics are being covered by the "Internet's Water Cooler" as they are being discussed. (Twitter is frequently described as the "Internet's Water Cooler" because it serves the same function as the water cooler in a break room in a traditional office—it gives co-workers a chance to share little snippets of their lives, including what they are working on right now.)

The hashtag can work the same way for an event that you host! A book club at your library could pick a hashtag and post some promotional discussion points about the upcoming book with this tag in the tweet. During the discussion, a staff member or volunteer could summarize the discussion in quick posts to Twitter, using the hashtag again. After the event, participants could continue the discussion just by posting a tweet with the hashtag included. All of this would be available to people who might be interested in the book but not able to make it to the physical event—and it would be good marketing and promotion for the book club as well.

One thing to keep in mind when choosing a hashtag is whether it has been used before. A quick search of Twitter will tell you if someone else is already using this particular tag for another reason. In that case, keep trying to find a tag that is short (they do count as part of the 140-character limit for each tweet) and unique so that your patrons aren't confused by unrelated conversations happening in the same hashtag space.

Another recent addition to Twitter's grouping features is Twitter Lists. Twitter announced the lists on September 30 in a blog post at http://blog.twitter.com/2009/09/soon-to-launch-lists.html. Lists give Twitter users a way to create groups of other Twitter users and share them. There are other options for creating lists, however. One is TweepML (http://tweepml.org), which also allows you to create lists of Twitter accounts that can then be easily shared and followed (in part or the whole thing) with a single click of a button. See Figure 3.4 for an example of one of the librarian Twitter lists on TweepML.

▶ Figure 3.4: Librarian List Created by TweepML

FriendFeed, on the other hand, does have a specific feature, Groups (formerly known as Rooms), that allows groups to form on its service. Groups are easy-to-create group building tools for FriendFeed. To create a group, go to www.friendfeed.com/groups/search and click the link on that page to "Create a group." (Once you have created the group, you can populate it by adding feeds from a blog, a social network like LibraryThing or Goodreads—both book-focused social sites—or from a search of the hashtag that you are using for your event in Twitter.) All Twitter searches produce an RSS feed, so this is an easy way to include the Twitter conversation in your FriendFeed room.

When you first create the group, you are asked to come up with a name. This name will be the URL of the group, so pick something short and memorable! You can choose the privacy level—if you want it completely open to anyone, completely private, or somewhere in between—and invite FriendFeed users to join the group immediately. Once you answer all of the questions, you submit the information and are taken directly to your new group. Here you can import various feeds to start populating the group with content or invite others to join, if you missed anyone, or wanted to wait and get some content before you started inviting folks.

FriendFeed's groups are more permanent than Twitter's hashtags, so they are great for ongoing programs—like the book club mentioned earlier—or for regular events at your library. If you have a large enough population on Twitter/FriendFeed and a group where you discuss your events, programs, and services, it could become a busy place! A completely open, public group also allows its members to invite new members, so your participants can become part of your marketing team. As their friends and relatives join these social networks, they can invite them into your group to discover all of the things that your organization is doing.

▶ LEARN TO USE THE SEARCH FEATURES

If you want to use any social network effectively, you need to learn how to use its search features. Searching for local users, for user groups that may be interested in what you have to say—or that may be interesting to your organization—and for mentions of your library will get you plenty to talk about in any social network. Both Twitter and FriendFeed have excellent search features that will help you find the people and topics that you will need to get your social community started.

How-to-Search Tips

▶ Twitter's search is at http://search.twitter.com (it can be hard to find otherwise).
▶ Both Twitter and FriendFeed have advanced search pages that can perform very specific searches on their data.
▶ Both Twitter and FriendFeed have limits to the archives that can be searched; those limits change occasionally, but you can't find Tweets or FriendFeed posts from a very long time ago using these search tools.
▶ Learn the search operators for each service (in FriendFeed they are below the advanced search form; in Twitter they are linked from the advanced search page).
▶ Use Boolean search strategies: The symbols + (plus) and – (minus) both work on FriendFeed and Twitter.
▶ Twitter's results now come up in regular Google or Bing searches, so you can use a regular search engine to access them!

How to Find People on Twitter

Twitter's search engine is based on a formerly third-party service called Summize that Twitter purchased and folded into its own offerings. Summize did such a great job of real-time searching of Twitter that the company decided to just buy it up rather than try to build the same sort of features into its own search. You can find the Twitter search page at http://search.twitter.com. It is similar to Google's search in that it has a single box that accepts search terms and a big button to press to perform the search. To get to the advanced search interface, you can click the "Advanced Search" link just below the search box.

Entering a phrase, word, or hashtag into the search box will give you a result page that automatically updates. The query is periodically re-sent and a box appears above the results telling you how many new results have been found since you started the search. You can easily refresh the page to see a conversation happening in almost real time. The search result page also lists "nifty queries" that let you know what other people are searching for from the Twitter search page. At the top of the page are both the RSS feed for the query—so you can continue following the conversation via your feed reader—and a link to let you send a tweet about the results to Twitter, effectively starting a metaconversation about the conversation.

All of this is available from the general search box. You can use this box to find people on Twitter, but if you want to narrow your results, follow the "Advanced Search" link to a form to do searches from a person, to a person, or referencing a person. This page, as well as the tools in "Find Locals" later in this chapter, is the best way to find individuals on Twitter.

How to Find Topics on Twitter

Another feature that Twitter offers on its search page is a list of the "Trending Topics." These are words, phrases, and hashtags that are showing up in many tweets. They are an excellent way to keep an eye on what people on Twitter are talking about. Anytime Google's Gmail goes down, you can instantly tell what is going on by the conversation on Twitter—the word "Gmail" generally shows up in the Trending Topics list within a few minutes of any outage. While local libraries are not likely to generate the buzz that a worldwide outage of Gmail would, you can still follow the trends and see what people are talking about in general. These might make interesting topics for you to tweet about yourself!

Using the Twitter search for hashtags gives you a look at what is being discussed even if the topic isn't big enough to make it to the Trending Topics list. If you are following a conference, such as the DrupalCon conference for the users of the popular Content Management System Drupal (www.drupal.org) that took place in early March 2009, you can enter the hashtag #drupalcon into Twitter's search and follow along with the conversation directly from the search page—or you can add the feed to your feed reader, too. All of this is useful on a personal level to see what people are talking about on Twitter, but it can also be very useful on an organizational level to see who is talking about your library and what they are talking about!

How to Keep Up with What People Are Saying on Twitter about Your Library

The first way to keep up with what people are saying is to do a keyword search on your library's name or on your town. You may be surprised to learn that there is a conversation going on in Twitter that directly affects you and your organization. Doing a basic keyword search at the Twitter search page is one way to find the conversation. Another way is to use a third-party application such as Tweetdeck (www.tweetdeck.com). Tweetdeck is a cross-platform (Mac, Linux, and Windows) application that gives you columns of tweets so that you can keep an eye on your regular tweet stream, your replies, and your direct messages. Another search column gives you real-time results for any search term(s) you enter into the search box on Tweetdeck. Just these four columns can make keeping up with your library's Twitter account and keeping an eye on what people are saying about your library very convenient.

How to Back Up and Archive Your Twitter Account

Twitter keeps only a few days of information available through searches, so if you want to keep track of what you have said in the past, or what others have said in the past, a backup copy of your account or an archive of search terms, hashtags, or other people's public accounts is necessary. To back up your own account, you can use a service like Tweetscan Backup (www.tweetscan.com/data.php) that will download your tweets, @replies, friends and followers, direct messages, and favorite tweets. The service is not completely free. It's currently priced at $1.99 per download, unless you are willing to tweet about using it—in that case it is free.

Another option, also not free, is Lifestream Backup (http://lifestreambackup.com). It has a 15-day free trial, so you can try it before you commit to paying for it. It will back up Twitter, Google

Docs, Delicious, Wordpress.com accounts, FriendFeed, and more. For some libraries, this may be worth paying a relatively small amount to have access to all of your information.

Finally, there is a program that is available called The Archivist (http://flotzam.com/archivist) that will run on your system and save all of your tweets as they happen. As of this writing, it is available only for the Windows operating system, but it is free. Tweetscan Backup, Lifestream Backup, and The Archivist are only three of the options that are available for you to use to back up your Twitter or FriendFeed accounts.

Backup Options

The Archivist (http://flotzam.com/archivist/): Windows desktop application that backs up Tweets to a local computer for free.

Backupify (formerly Lifestream Backup; www.backupify.com): Backs up Twitter for free and others (including Facebook, Gmail, and Google Docs) for a monthly fee depending on the amount of storage needed.

SocialSafe (http://socialsafe.net): Includes status updates so that your tweets sent to Facebook will be backed up; not free—pricing varies.

TwapperKeeper (http://twapperkeeper.com): Backs up all tweets with a given hashtag for free.

Tweetbackup (http://tweetbackup.com/): Free, daily backups of your Twitter account.

Tweetscan Backup (www.tweetscan.com/data.php): Twitter backups of the last 1,000 messages, with payment each time or free with an advertising tweet sent from your account.

Twistory (http://twistory.net): Imports tweets for free into supported calendars (including Google Calendar and Outlook) for backup/archiving purposes.

How to Search FriendFeed

FriendFeed also has a convenient search box located right on the top of just about every page you go to in the site. While the regular search box is handy for quick lookups, the Advanced Search feature, found at www.friendfeed.com/search/advanced, is incredibly powerful for finding nuggets of information that might otherwise be buried in FriendFeed. The advanced search interface includes these elements:

- ▶ Title
- ▶ Comments
- ▶ Shared from site
- ▶ Shared by
- ▶ In the group
- ▶ Commented on by
- ▶ Liked by
- ▶ Has at least [you fill in desired number of] comments
- ▶ Has at least [you fill in desired number of] likes

With these search operators available, you can find something in the comments that might be quite difficult to find in a quick scan of your FriendFeed page. You can also use this search interface to look inside of any public group (use the operator—group: lsw) or to see posts that generated the most comments on a particular subject (has at least ___ # of comments). You can see what your friends liked (liked by) and you can find anything that others have shared from a particular service (use the operator—service: *twitter*). All of these options make FriendFeed a gold mine of information and conversations in which you can participate.

How to Search Tumblr

Tumblr has a basic search box on the top right of every page on the site, but it also has an "Explore" section that gives you more options for finding things on Tumblr. To do a basic search, you enter a keyword or two into the search box and hit Enter. The results page is interesting—the results are presented as square tiles with a bit of text from the text-based post, the image from a photo post or text, and a screenshot from a video post. Clicking any of the tiles takes you to the page that contained your keyword(s). You can also use the drop-down arrow just behind the magnifying glass to change what you are searching: the whole site, your dashboard, your posts, or Tumblr's help pages.

The Explore section lets you browse the site to find things in different, often more visual ways:

- ▶ **Radar**: What's new and popular on Tumblr now.
- ▶ **Directory**: Staff picks of the best and most interesting posts, what has been on the radar recently that the staff really liked, popular themes that have been uploaded to use with a Tumblog, and more.
- ▶ **Trends**: A feature that lets you compare the relative popularity of any four keywords across the Tumblr blogs.
- ▶ **Map**: Find local Tumblrs using the Map, or just watch where each new post is coming from as it is posted.
- ▶ **Themes**: Many different themes for you to use in your Tumblr blog.

▶ DOWNLOAD HELPER APPLICATIONS

Many different third-party applications can make your Friend-Feed/Twitter experience much easier and more convenient. Developers create these applications using the APIs that each of the sites makes available. The third-party application landscape changes frequently, so be sure to check with the directories of applications for each site that are included in the Recommended Resources chapter of this book to see what new applications developers have added since this book was written. The good thing about each of these applications that I will present in this section is that they are completely free to download, install, and use. However, if you want to support the development of new and better applications, you can generally donate some cash to the developers to keep innovative new programs coming.

Make Twitter Work for You

Two of the more popular desktop applications are available using the Adobe Air platform (www.adobe.com/products/air). Adobe

Air is a development platform that helps to produce and run applications that will work on Windows, Linux, and the Mac OS operating systems. Because it is so easy to produce applications that are compatible with multiple operating systems using this development toolbox, many of the desktop applications that you will find for Twitter and FriendFeed require Adobe Air. There is a download and install process for the Air platform—which most Air applications will handle when you are installing them—and then there are occasional updates that you should apply as well. This may be an issue if you do not have software installation rights on your computer.

Twhirl (www.twhirl.org) and Tweetdeck (www.tweetdeck.com) are two applications that use Adobe's Air platform to improve and extend your Twitter experience. Twhirl works with several different services, to give you a single, unified interface:

- ▶ Twitter
- ▶ StatusNet (and Identi.ca)
- ▶ FriendFeed
- ▶ Seesmic (a social video-sharing service)

You can follow your "information stream" from any of the services listed as well as post new status updates, shorten URLs for use in Twitter and StatusNet, and search any of the services from one application interface. Twhirl also has a feature that allows you to save any search you perform from its application to get almost real-time updates for those search terms as they are published.

Tweetdeck is similar, enhancing and allowing manipulation of your Twitter stream. Although it was limited to just the Twitter service at first, it will now work with Facebook status updates as well. Tweetdeck takes your Twitter stream and splits it into panes—one for your personal Twitter timeline, one for replies to your Twitter account, and another for Direct Messages to you. You can then create groups of people you subscribe to—perhaps all of the librarians you follow on Twitter—and have just their tweets show up in yet another pane. You can save searches and get the results displayed in still another pane on the application. Tweetdeck offers robust filtering options that will let you pull out just the tweets you want from any particular stream very quickly.

For those of us in the United States, Twitter is easily accessible through the SMS text messaging application on mobile phones. Outside of the United States, though, Twitter currently does not support text message sending or receiving. One of the mobile Twitter applications listed at the Twitter Fan Wiki, though, will give you SMS capabilities outside of the United States (http://twe2 .com). Other mobile applications do everything from basic Twitter functions to very specific applications that will pull scores from games to your phone via the Twitter service or give exact GPS coordinates of where you are when you are tweeting. Because of the number of operating systems used in mobile phones, you will need to check any application out before you download it to make sure it will work with your setup. Check out the "Find New Helper Applications" section later in this chapter to get pointers to lists of mobile applications for your phone.

Another area where third-party applications are helpful is in URL shortening. Because some Web addresses are so long that they would take over a 140-character message, leaving little room for anything else, a class of applications has become very popular to use with Twitter and FriendFeed. There are several options, but the one that I use is bit.ly (www.bit.ly), which adds some value to the act of making URLs shorter. It offers URL tracking services that can tell you how often a shortened link has been clicked. You can either sign up for a free account to track information or just keep track of the short links and add a + sign to the end of them to see the statistics that bit.ly provides. A shortened URL looks like http://bit.ly/zCpCh (which goes to twitter.com). To find the statistics on how many have used this URL, you would just type in http://bit.ly/zCpCh+ into your Web browser and get the information. bit.ly is included in the Tweetdeck application as one of the options for URL shorteners, and it is a popular choice with other clients and third-party applications as well.

TwitThis (http://twitthis.com) is another service that includes a feature to shorten URLs. With TwitThis, however, you can take the code for the service and easily insert it into your Web site or blog template. This gives visitors to your site or blog a way to immediately tweet the link to your content from your page—they do not have to go to their Twitter client or the Twitter homepage first—so sharing your content is made very easy.

One thing to consider when using a URL shortener, however, is the fact that a lot of hackers use them to hide links to virus-laden sites and phishing schemes and other undesirable Web sites. Twitter has begun filtering bad links from its service, but as of this writing, it does not expand shortened URLs to check them. You can avoid problems by installing a Firefox plug-in like LongURL (http://longurl.org/tools).

There are also browser helpers available for Twitter, such as the TwitterBar (www.chrisfinke.com/addons/twitterbar) Firefox extension. TwitterBar puts an icon in your Firefox address bar that gives you the ability to post tweets directly from that bar (see Figures 3.5 and 3.6 for examples of what TwitterBar looks like in action).

Get the Most Out of FriendFeed

FriendFeed also has a number of helper applications that make using the service easier and more convenient. The simplest way to improve the usability of FriendFeed is to install the FriendFeed bookmarklet (http://friendfeed.com/share/bookmarklet). This little bit of code creates a link in your browser's link bar that, when clicked, will automatically post the page you are viewing to FriendFeed. This makes sharing sites much easier even than copying and pasting a link into the "post" box on FriendFeed's homepage. Once you've clicked the link, you can choose which room

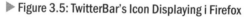
▶ Figure 3.5: TwitterBar's Icon Displaying i Firefox

▶ Figure 3.6: TwitterBar's Options Opens When You Hover the Cursor Above the TwitterBar Icon

you would like to post the site to, what images you would like to post (just click on an image on the page and it will automatically be added to your post), and add a comment to the post before it is sent to FriendFeed. While posting normally on FriendFeed is not all that hard, this makes it much more convenient for you—you can post as you are already surfing around the Net.

Another convenience tool that FriendFeed offers is Mail2FF (http://friendfeed.com/share/mail). When you go to the Mail2FF site, you will see an e-mail address made up of your username and Remote Key that you can use to post things to FriendFeed from your e-mail (or your SMS/e-mail–enabled phone). To post something to a specific room in FriendFeed, you add the room name before your username and send it in! Another tool that FriendFeed offers is a Facebook application. After you install the application in your Facebook account, it displays your FriendFeed posts within Facebook. The Post to Twitter application posts your FriendFeed activity to your Twitter account. You get granular controls as to what goes on Twitter—all posts to public rooms, comments and likes that you make—and you can choose which services you would like to have re-posted to Twitter, just in case you are feeding some of the RSS feeds into Twitter already, such as your blog's RSS or Facebook's status updates.

Twhirl, described earlier in detail, is another helper application that will display your FriendFeed stream on your desktop in almost real time. If you are away from your desktop, however, and have a Web-enabled phone, you can use fftogo (www.fftogo.com) to read and post to your FriendFeed account. It is optimized for use with slow cell phone connections and tiny screens and is very helpful if you are trying to keep a conversation going while away from your computer.

Find New Helper Applications

One of the best ways to find new helper applications with Twitter or FriendFeed is to pay attention to your information streams from the applications themselves. Every tweet that is posted to the service has a small "tag" on it that identifies where the post originated. Some will say "from txt," meaning that the post came from an SMS application on a cell phone; others will give the name of an application, such as Twhirl or Tweetdeck. The Web interface to Twitter makes each of the names of the helper applications clickable—and if the tweet has come from a text messaging service, the word "txt" will link to the help pages explaining what commands can be used from SMS.

On FriendFeed, many people will post about what applications they like and are using with the service occasionally, so you can stumble upon things this way. You can also do a quick search for "FriendFeed applications" and see what people are talking about right now. In addition, a public room in FriendFeed is devoted to discussing FriendFeed applications; called "We Love Apps" (www .friendfeed.com/room/weloveapps), it may help you find a new application that will make your use of FriendFeed effortless. A blog post that may help you find a good application for your FriendFeed needs is a roundup of desktop applications for FriendFeed called "7 Desktop Applications for FriendFeed," originally posted at Mashable (http://mashable.com/2008/10/01/ desktop-applications-for-friendfeed). At the beginning of this post are links to even more lists of applications that are useful with FriendFeed. A quick search of the Internet will pull up even more examples of applications that can keep you productive in your use of FriendFeed.

▶ BUILD AN ONLINE COMMUNITY

While FriendFeed, Twitter, Tumblr, Identi.ca, and all of the other microblogging and lifestreaming services that I have discussed are great ways to get your message out, they really shine when you use them as conversational tools, not as broadcasts. When you watch for comments about your library, or for questions that local folks are asking, and answer those questions or respond to those comments, you are starting a conversation. This conversation can become the building blocks of a digital community that is based upon your organization. You can do, with Twitter or FriendFeed, the same sort of community outreach and community events that you do with your on-site programs. Using these tools to create a community of people who are thinking of the library as their information resource, you can improve the way your patrons feel about their local library.

Make Friends

The point to using social networks is to network with your peers in a social setting. You have to make friends on the various services for them to be of any use to you at all. Some services, such as Facebook, are set up to make finding and connecting to friends very, very easy. Others, like Twitter, make it a bit harder. Both Twitter and FriendFeed make the possibility of stumbling across people who are a Friend of a Friend (FOAF) easy—Twitter with their reply feature and FriendFeed with their FOAF feature that shows FriendFeeders with whom your friends are engaging in conversation. Both methods allow you to find people who your friends know and talk to in an organic manner. This method is somewhat hit or miss, though, and will not necessarily get you the number of friends and contacts that your administration might like to see. When you are just starting with a Twitter or FriendFeed account, using the tools to follow others will ensure that you at least find as many local friends and contacts as possible. After you have found all of the locals you can, then you can start to work on getting them to follow you back.

Because most of the traffic seems to be heading to Twitter and to FriendFeed, they have the best tools available for use of their services. I will focus on these two services for the rest of the book, but do not forget that there are other services out there that your particular community may be using more than either Twitter or FriendFeed.

Find Locals

There are several ways to find local "tweeters" in the Twitterverse. One that is useful is the TwitterLocal application (www.twitterlocal .net). This application allows you to filter tweets by location. You enter a city or ZIP code and a radius (within 5, 10, 15, etc., miles) and it will give you a real-time feed of all the tweets that are coming from folks with that location in the location field of their Twitter account. This will give you only active Twitterers, though, not a list of everyone that gives a location within your search area. Keeping an eye on the tweet stream for a few days should give you a good idea of who is twittering and what they are tweeting about. This is a good way to keep an eye on your local conversation. As a resource and information provider, you can offer resources and information over Twitter just as easily as you can through blog comments or e-mail responses, and you might just impress your audience enough to get them to follow you back.

Another way to find local Twitterers is to use the Twellow (www.twellow.com) directory. It is like a phone directory for Twitter folks, but it also searches by location, as well as by name and what content of biographies. Enter a location into the search box at the top of the Twellow Web site, and you will get a list of all the Twitterers who claim that location in their profile. Unlike TwitterLocal, you cannot just put in a ZIP code and get everyone within a certain radius—you will have to search on a city name or state. Even so, the search is pretty easy, and the results are for everyone in that area, not just folks who have tweeted recently.

To find locals in the FriendFeed service, you can use FriendFeed's own search page. Unlike Twitter, FriendFeed does not really have a profile that you fill out, so there are no easy ways to find location in FriendFeed. You can do searches for locations and see who is posting from various points on the globe. You can also use the Twitter FriendFeed finder (https://friendfeed.com/settings/import/twitter) to see if any of the local people you are following on Twitter are also on FriendFeed. From there you can also follow those locals on FriendFeed. FriendFeed also has an excellent FOAF service that pulls comments and posts from friends of people you already consider friends into your feed. You can sometimes find local folks this way, as well.

Friending on Twitter

The mechanics of "making friends" (friending) in Twitter is pretty simple. When you log into your account, and you visit another Twitterer's page, you will see a "Follow" button below that person's picture. Pressing that button is all you need to do to become a follower. If the account is public, you are done—all of the person's tweets will show up in your Twitter stream, and you will be following his or her updates along with those of your other friends on Twitter. If the account is private, the person will get a message that you are requesting to be a follower. If the person approves, you will start seeing his or her tweets in your stream. If the person does not approve, the account will remain private and you will not be able to see any of the posts. Either way, even if you are approved as a follower, the person might decide not to follow you back. Twitter defines a "follower" as someone who is getting the updates of a Twitter user but is not being followed by that account in return. "Friends" in Twitter are accounts that follow each other.

That is pretty much all there is to the process of following people on Twitter. There is much more to consider, however, than just the act of clicking the "Follow" button. You should decide on a "following policy." Some libraries wait until they are followed, thinking it is creepy to have an organization follow real people. Others follow everyone who fits their criteria, and others are somewhere in between.

As the person who manages the Twitter account for my library, I fall on the "follow everyone local I can" side of the debate. As I mentioned before, the people you follow do not have to follow you back, and most people with a public account are prepared to share their updates with anyone who cares to read them.

There are more decisions to make, once you have decided whether your library will actively follow local members of your community or not. When other people follow your account, you will need to make a decision about whether or not you will follow them back. Some organizations follow everyone who follows them—they are friendly, but they could become overwhelmed with the number of updates in their tweet stream. Other libraries treat Twitter as a broadcast medium and do not follow anyone at all. This defeats the purpose of using a social application that is good at creating conversations, however. Still other libraries will follow people who live in their general service area or attend their parent college or university. This can be a good way to foster communication while still keeping the number of status updates they get from their friends to a manageable level. This can sometimes be difficult if Twitterers do not put their exact locations in their profiles.

When I asked on FriendFeed what the library staff who manage library Twitter accounts do when it comes to following other people with their library Twitter accounts, I got several responses. Josh Neff, a Web Content Developer for the Johnson County Library in Kansas, said that, "I follow anyone who looks genuine & could potentially have a conversation with us. If it looks like a business just shooting links out, I won't follow them."

Jenny Levine, who manages the Twitter account for the American Library Association (ALA), said, "For the ALA conference accounts, we didn't start out following anyone because we didn't have the resources to monitor and respond to conversations, and we didn't want to raise expectations. However, we've been able to take advantage of the RSS feeds and Twitter search to resolve that, and now we follow most who follow us, except the obvious marketers. I'm really glad we've been able to move in this direction, and we're working on something that will make this even easier."

Laura Norvig, the Resource Center Coordinator for ETR Associates, described a slightly different approach. She said in her response to my question that, "I've been protective and guarded about who I follow (I'm tweeting for our overall online Resource Center, but similar concept to a library), reasoning that who I follow is a recommendation, so I've stuck to orgs mostly, which also gives me a great informative feed. But I do see how not following individuals stifles my chance to converse with them. I'm torn."

Finally, Andrew Shuping, the ILL/Circulation Services Librarian for the Jack Tarver Library at Mercer University in Macon, Georgia, said that, "I just recently decided to follow a few folks, mostly ones that were library related such as other libraries or the nytbook or a couple of bigger publishers. I also followed a couple of people that have/had a connection to the library." You can see from these responses that there is no one accepted way to structure your following policies. You can follow everyone, no one, or any combination between!

Friending on FriendFeed

Becoming someone's friend on FriendFeed is easy, too. When you hover your mouse over the name of a person on FriendFeed, a bubble of information pops up, giving you the person's avatar, statistics (how many likes, comments, etc., he or she made in the past), and a link to subscribe, if you do not already. Once you click that "Subscribe" link, the person will get an e-mail that you are now a follower. The person can then choose to follow you back, ignore the fact that you are a follower, or block you so that you cannot see his or her updates, even if he or she has a public profile.

As with Twitter, the mechanics of friending or following people in FriendFeed is the easy part. What policies you have in place to deal with who and what you friend, follow, ignore, or block is the difficult part.

Create a Community with Twitter

The best way to create a community using the Twitter application is to start using it regularly. Watch your tweet stream on a regular basis. Run searches on your library's name, and respond to comments and questions as soon as possible. Contribute information that is relevant to both you and your community—make yourself useful! Once people in your area start to realize that their local library is on Twitter, paying attention to their tweets, and engaged in the overall conversation, you will begin to notice that you are referenced in more tweets, asked more questions, and offered more comments. The community will begin to grow.

Feed Your Community with FriendFeed/Tumblr

Once you have a community in place, you can feed it with regular posts. Post about anything that is happening in your organization—or about the weather if necessary. On a slow day at the Missouri River Regional Library, I once posted a tweet that just said, "it's cold outside, but warm in the library—stop by and read a magazine in our toasty warm reading room!" Anything that you post will add to the possibilities of conversation for your community. Some ideas for posting follow:

- ▶ Events and programs
- ▶ New services
- ▶ News stories about your library

- ▶ New staff
- ▶ Special awards or honors given to library staff
- ▶ Events sponsored by partner organizations
- ▶ Important local information
- ▶ Library announcements and special news
- ▶ "Retweets" of any of the above from those you follow

The possibilities are limitless—anything that comes to mind as something people should know about your library is fair game for posting to Twitter and FriendFeed.

Follow Community-Building Best Practices

One thing to keep in mind as you are building your community is the fact that people are busy. While you want to get the word out about your organization, you also don't want to flood either Twitter or FriendFeed with a bunch of posts from your library. A scheduled posting service like FutureTweets (http://futuretweets.com) or SocialOomph (www.socialoomph.com) will help you balance out your tweets. Another thing to remember is that the Internet thrives on the "gift economy" of giving attention and notice to others (for further discussion of the gift economy, see Wikipedia's article at http://en.wikipedia.org/wiki/Gift_Economy; accessed March 23, 2009). Highlight what other libraries in your area are doing. Point out what other service organizations are working on now. Give other organizations attention and notice, and it will come back to you!

One way to give to the community—and increase the information you provide to your followers and friends—is to "retweet" other people's tweets. The idea is that you resend out a tweet from someone you follow to the people who follow you—with attribution—and thereby give both more information to your followers and the gift of attention to the original tweeter.

Other things to think about are the cultural norms of the services. Twitter and FriendFeed have definite cultures that have grown up around their use. If you violate one of these norms, you may find yourself losing followers—and a place in the front of their minds of your patrons—because of it. The best way to discover the cultural norms of Twitter and FriendFeed is to watch the conversation, discover people's expectations of responses, and pay attention to the "normal" way people ask questions, give responses, and give thanks for any help they get.

Jason Griffey, the head of IT for the University of Tennessee in Chattanooga, said in a FriendFeed comment that one cultural norm for Twitter is the act of giving credit to the original Twitter user when retweeting. Violating this norm when retweeting can make your organization look like either a clueless user or one that is more concerned with its image than with helping others—and one standard of the Twitter community (and libraries) is to help others while you are participating!

Sidebar: Social Media Norms

Twitter
- ▶ Don't follow and then immediately unfollow people.
- ▶ Use Twitter for public conversations—don't bore the rest of your followers with a private conversation that should be conducted via IM.
- ▶ Use hashtags responsibly—don't abuse their powers!
- ▶ Don't ask for retweets—if your content is good, it will be retweeted.

FriendFeed
- ▶ Don't flood the stream with the same thing posted to multiple social sites—fine-tune your settings to remove duplicates from your stream.

Both
- ▶ Don't use either service just for promotional posts—be human and engage in conversation.
- ▶ Give credit when you reuse other people's content.
- ▶ Friend others wisely—make sure you can get value from their stream and don't be offended if they decide that they won't get value from yours and don't follow you back.

▶4

MARKETING

- ▶ **Get the Word Out**
- ▶ **Incorporate Twitter/Tumblr/FriendFeed into Your Marketing Strategy**
- ▶ **Manage Your Brand**
- ▶ **Organize Your Information Streams**
- ▶ **Promote Your Library**

Libraries have traditionally marketed themselves using book-marks, flyers, and word of mouth. Some libraries have ventured into newspaper advertisements and radio or television spots to try to reach people who do not normally come into the library. Media ads can be expensive, though, and they still might not reach the people you want to reach. If you are aiming toward a younger audience, those in their early 20s to early 40s, you may find that they do not read the newspaper, watch television commercials, or listen to the radio in the car. There is a good chance that folks in this age group get their news from the Internet, fast forward through commercials with their DVRs (Digital Video Recorders) such as TiVo, and listen to their MP3 players as they drive around.

What many people in this age group do, however, is spend a good deal of time communicating online. They check their Facebook accounts for status updates and catch up on their friends' lives through Twitter or FriendFeed. If your organization has a presence online, these people are much more likely to run across your information than if you publish it in the newspaper or talk about it on the radio. This is very much a case of "being where your users are" so that you can let them know what is going on without making them feel like you are advertising to them.

▶ GET THE WORD OUT

Be Where Your Users Are

A big part of the Library 2.0 movement has been to focus on where our users are and then try to be there at their point of need. Many libraries have public computers—this is a great way to find out what your local population prefers. If many people in the computer center are visiting FriendFeed, then you definitely need a presence there—and the same with Tumblr and Twitter. This makes it more likely that your users will find you and find the information that you are providing through these Web 2.0 services.

Use Twitter to Reach Your Audience

Getting the word out with Twitter can be challenging, because you are limited to 140 characters per post. To get the most out of the limited amount of space you have for a particular tweet, think of each of your posts as a part of the whole "body" of postings that you are putting out there. Consider the posts in aggregate—what they say about your library as a whole—as well as individual snippets of information. If your posts have a consistent structure and focus, this will help brand your library and will make your Twitter stream more useful for others.

The MarketingProfs Daily Fix Blog (www.mpdailyfix.com/2007/09/7_ways_marketers_can_use_twitt.html) posted seven ways that marketers can use Twitter to their advantage:

1. Twitter extends the reach to those individuals or companies that already have a blogging strategy in place and want to deepen or further ties.

2. Retailers can announce sales and deals (for libraries, this could be new materials, new promotions such as Missouri River Regional Library's Food for Fines food drive, or other special events that patrons may want to know about).

3. Twitter increases the ability for frequent updates to blogs or Web sites or news.

4. It builds consensus or a community of supporters.

5. It builds buzz.

6. It enables you to update breaking news at conferences or events.

7. It enables you to shape your network to reflect your own personal branding.

This marketing Web site (www.mpdailyfix.com) gives examples of each of these in practice, if you would like some more information about any of these ways to use Twitter for your library.

Use FriendFeed and Tumblr to Reach Your Audience

To best catch the attention of people who are already online, use one of the many widgets that FriendFeed and Tumblr provide to make your information available to a wide variety of community and organizational Web sites.

FriendFeed

1. Log into your FriendFeed account.

2. Scroll to the bottom of the page and click on "Tools & Widgets."

3. Click on "Embeddable Widgets."

4. Click on "Feed Widget."

5. Customize it with the feed you want to display, services you want to include, number of posts to display in the widget, and the functions you want to show (logo, numbers of comments and likes, and a "Subscribe" link) in the widget.

6. Choose the format (JavaScript or Image—JavaScript will not work on some blogging platforms such as WordPress, but it is more interactive than a static image of your widget).

7. Under the "More Options" link you can also set the width of the badge if you need it to fit a particular space on your site.

8. Copy the HTML that is in the box below the customization form.

9. Paste it into the Web page you want to display the widget on.

This is the process to take the FriendFeed widget and reuse all of the information you are feeding into the service.

Tumblr

Tumblr has a widget that you can install in your blog or Web page in much the same way.

1. Go to your Tumblr dashboard.

2. Click on "Account, Goodies."

3. Scroll to "Embed Your Tumblog."

4. Copy the code into this box.

5. Paste the code into an HTML page or a blog widget.

6. Enjoy!

Besides the widget, you can also use the RSS to populate your Twitter stream or do any number of things that will get your message out and get people informed about what you are doing. Now that you have let people who are already using the services know that you are there, and you have begun the process of creating a community with those people, it is time to start promoting your new Twitter or FriendFeed accounts or letting people know about your new tumblog. This is a never-ending process—you will want a permanent spot on your library's bookmarks for your Twitter address or a sign in your library that directs interested users to your Tumblr or FriendFeed account.

▶ INCORPORATE TWITTER/TUMBLR/FRIENDFEED INTO YOUR MARKETING STRATEGY

Put your Twitter address or your Tumblr blog URL on everything: link to it from your homepage, add it to your bookmarks, include it in event flyers, and mention it at any tech-related programs and especially at programs that are targeted for younger patrons. Create connections between all of your social networking sites—add your Twitter stream to your Facebook page, or include your tumblog as a sidebar in your main blog.

The best way to get the word out about anything your library is doing—Twitter, FriendFeed, and Tumblr included—is to educate your staff. Make sure your public relations or marketing staff know what your Twitter, Tumblr, or FriendFeed account is for, and they might be able to come up with ways to market it that you had not considered. Keep your front desk staff informed, and they will be able to refer people to the appropriate account when patrons come to them for information. Make sure that your Web content folks are aware of what can—and cannot—be included in your Twitter stream, your Tumblr blog, or your FriendFeed account, and they may be able to provide you with content you would not be aware of otherwise. Staff involvement—even if the staff will never touch a social networking account on their own—is key to getting the right information sent your way and the right patrons informed about what you are doing.

Strategy Paper

You may want to write out a "strategy paper" that explains the overall goal of your social networking efforts. It should list each social network you are part of and what the goals are for that individual network. This can be a great tool for getting other staff members aware of what your organization's social networks are doing for you and what they can do for your social networks!

Let the World Know What You Are Doing with Twitter/FriendFeed/Tumblr

Princeton University's WordNet Web site (http://wordnetweb .princeton.edu/perl/webwn?s=widget) defines a widget as "a device or control that is very useful for a particular job" and gives several synonyms, including doodad, gizmo, and doohickey (all of which I've heard in reference to these widgets). On the Web, a widget is a microapplication that takes code from one site and displays it on another. Twitter, FriendFeed, and Tumblr all make widgets (sometimes also referred to as "badges" on various sites) available for your use from their site. This is an excellent way to extend the reach of the information you post to these sites as well as a great way to promote your account on the various sites. Be sure to look for widgets or badges on any social networking site that you use, and then use them liberally on your Web sites and social networks and promote them for use by community organizations.

Most widgets are copy-and-paste, easy to install applications. If you have a Web page that is created with HTML or a blog that is run by any of the major blog providers (Blogger, WordPress, TypePad, etc.), you can easily take the code that the site provides, copy it into your site, and reuse the information you post to Twitter, Tumblr, or FriendFeed very easily.

Wordpress.com is one of the fastest-growing blog sites around, and, if you choose to host your own blog, you will probably use the open source, self-hosted version available from wordpress.org. Below are the steps to install a FriendFeed widget into the sidebar of a Wordpress.com blog. The steps will be the same for a self-hosted blog and very similar for any other type of blog—even easier for a static HTML page.

1. From the WordPress dashboard, click on "Appearance ◊ Widgets."
2. Find the Text widget and click the word "Add" next to it.
3. Click on the "Edit" link at the right of the new widget that appears on your page.
4. Go to FriendFeed and click on the "Tools & Widgets" link, and choose the "Embeddable Widgets" link.
5. Choose the widget or badge that you prefer; for this example, I will use the Feed widget.
6. Customize the feed using the drop-down menus and check boxes on the left.
7. Note the choice of JavaScript or Image formats—many externally hosted blogs, such as Wordpress.com, do not allow

JavaScript on their sites because of security concerns. In that case, choose the Image option.

8. Copy the text in the "Copy and paste HTML" box.
9. Paste into your Wordpress.com Text widget box.
10. Click "Done" and then "Save Changes."
11. View your blog with your new widget in the sidebar.

For an HTML page that you manage, you can just copy the text from the "copy and paste HTML" box and copy it into any page at any place you would like the feed to appear. Upload or save the page, and the widget will be there!

Adding widgets and badges to your other Web sites increases the number of people who will see your information and helps spread the word about your Twitter, FriendFeed, or Tumblr account.

▶ MANAGE YOUR BRAND

Your "brand" online is your identity. Because many people who will interact with your library through Twitter or FriendFeed may have never come into your building to meet your smiling staff or see your spacious and comfy seating areas, this online brand is all they know of you. Branding your library consists of taking actions online that always keep in mind how you want your patrons to perceive your organization. Keep in mind that every post you make on any service is part of your "brand," and keep your message consistent. If you are promoting a particular event on your library's events blog, make note of it in your Twitter feed and post a blurb about it on your Tumblr blog.

Greg Schwartz, in his "Branding: Not Just for Cows Anymore" presentation at the Internet Librarian conference in 2008 (see www.slideshare.net/planetneutral/branding-not-just-for-cows-anymore-presentation), gave six tips for managing your online brand:

1. **Have a home base**. Most libraries have a Web site that they can point people to when they are referring to themselves online, but if you do not yet have one, get one!

2. **Own your username.** Try to get your library's name (or as close to it as possible) in every social networking site you can. Bè consistent!

3. **Aggregate your lifestream.** Make use of FriendFeed to put all of your various social networking sites' updates and posts together in one spot. For libraries that do not have a homepage, this aggregated stream would make a fine substitute.

4. **Join the conversation.** Post original content in Twitter, FriendFeed, or Tumblr. Comment on conversations that are relevant.

5. **Follow what others are saying about you.** Search Twitter, FriendFeed, and Google to see what people are saying about your library—and respond!

6. **Be authentic.** Allow a human voice to come through in your social networking conversations. Do not limit yourself to "organization speak," and do let staff post in their own "voice."

Keep your offline brand in mind while you are participating in social networks online. Use your logo as your avatar, and focus on the same events, topics, and concerns on Twitter and Tumblr as you do on your flyers and bookmarks. Consistency is key to maintaining your brand from a brick-and-mortar existence to a virtual one! Be sure to coordinate your Twitter or Tumblr posts with your public relations or marketing people so that you are giving patrons the same message and emphasizing the same issues in all of your media offerings.

▶ ORGANIZE YOUR INFORMATION STREAMS

The organization of social networking information streams is where FriendFeed really shines. FriendFeed gives you a single place in which to get all of the information put out by all of your friends at nearly all of the social networking sites out there. This makes FriendFeed valuable for both organizing your own information streams and for dealing with the occasionally overwhelming information streams that your well-connected friends and patrons produce.

One way to create an information stream that is both useful and usable is to place an imaginary friend in FriendFeed. The original concept of the imaginary friend was as a way to let people who use FriendFeed still get updates and information from people who do not use the service. A FriendFeed user can set up an imaginary friend by naming a feed, importing the public feed from any service (Facebook, Twitter, blogs, etc.) into that feed, and then subscribing to it.

The imaginary friend concept changed slightly in April 2009 with the release of a new version of FriendFeed. At that time the concept was melded with the concept of rooms to create "groups." You could create either a room or an imaginary friend using the new groups feature. To do this:

1. Click on "Browse/Edit Groups" in the Groups box on the right side of the page.

2. Click the "Create a Group" link at the top of the Groups page.

3. Give the group both a name and a username (the user name is what FriendFeed uses to create the custom URL for the group).

4. Choose between a private, standard, or public group:

   a. private group—a group that requires an invitation to join or subscribe and to post

   b. standard group—a group that allows only one person to post, but anyone can subscribe and comment to the posts

   c. public group—a completely open group that allows anyone to subscribe, post, and comment

5. Click the "Create Feed" button.

6. Start adding feeds to the group from the various social networking sites to which your "imaginary friend" belongs.

7. For libraries, this is a good way to get community organizations that may have a blog or a Facebook page, but no

FriendFeed account, into a single river of information on FriendFeed. Of course, once they are in FriendFeed, you can use the tools that FriendFeed provides to create a widget or badge of information from all of those community organizations (if you bundle them all up into one group) or from a single organization that you would like to follow but that does not have an account on the FriendFeed service. This is an excellent way to organize your community or larger organization's information into a single space that your library can then reuse and repurpose in multiple ways.

▶ PROMOTE YOUR LIBRARY

Spamming

To **spam** is defined in the *Oxford English Dictionary* as "To flood (a network, esp. the Internet, a newsgroup, or individuals) with a large number of unsolicited postings, or multiple copies of the same posting. Also intr.: to send large numbers of unsolicited messages or advertisements." Spamming on social networks is very similar. If all of your posts are just pointers to your resources, events, and pages, then you may be perceived as a spammer. If you flood the service with multiple posts about a particular event, you **will** be perceived as a spammer! Don't overwhelm your followers with too many messages about a particular service or event, and do point to what others in your community or area are doing as well. Sharing the events of others will, like karma, turn around and come back to you in good ways!

A major reason to get involved with the social networking sites, such as Twitter, FriendFeed, and Tumblr, is to let people know what is going on at your library. Of course, providing service to patrons is a major goal of any social networking outreach effort, but you also want to keep in mind that you are not only providing services, you are also giving people information about what your library is and what it can do for them. Remember that every social networking transaction, unlike a traditional circulation or reference transaction, is public and readable by anyone with an account on that service (or, in the case of Tumblr, anyone at all—whether or not they have an account). This is a good thing! Every question you answer via Twitter is archived and can be useful to far more people than just the single questioning patron. Every FriendFeed comment that you make can have value for the person making the original comment as well as all of their friends. Every Tumblr post you produce can be seen, enjoyed, and learned from by anyone with a computer and Internet access who cares to look. This is a powerful way to promote your library and the services your library provides.

The best way to promote your library is to get involved. If you start using Twitter with the intention of garnering attention for your organization, you may come off as a spammer. If, however, you use Twitter to augment your reference services, inform your patrons of events and programs, or create a dialogue with patrons, you will be much more authentic and other Twitter users are less likely to perceive you as a spammer.

Voice

Deciding on the "voice" that your Twitter, FriendFeed, or Tumblr account will use is vital to how you are going to promote your library. Take the time to ask yourself some questions:

- ▶ Is this an institutional account or an account of someone at an institution?
  - ➤ The institutional account will be the official "voice" of the institution, not reflective of any one person at that organization. It is more formal and less personal.
  - ➤ An account of someone at an institution will be the distinct "voice" of someone who works at the library. It is informal (unless this person is generally a formal communicator) and personable.
- ▶ Who will manage the account and the posters?
- ▶ If this is an institutional account, will there be one person posting? Will there be a backup if this person leaves or takes a vacation?

▶ If this is a person at your institution, is there more than one staff member posting "officially"? Will your organization's presence on the site dry up if this staff member gets busy, goes on vacation, or leaves the organization?

Each of these questions can be answered in a brief document outlining the style of the account and the rules for what is, and is not, fair game for posting. The time for creating this guide is during the planning phase—as you are deciding what the goals for the account are. But do not forget that this guide will also inform the staff of the voice of the institution across any of the social sites you are using. Consistency in voice is essential for creating your brand and effectively promoting your library. See the sidebar earlier in this chapter on the use of a strategy paper to get the information out and to your staff in another way.

▶5

BEST PRACTICES

▶ **Create Multiple Microblogging Accounts**

▶ **Comment and Post Often on Lifestreaming Accounts**

▶ **Manage Information Overload**

▶ **Avoid Social Network Spamming**

▶ **Keep Up with the Lingo**

FriendFeed, which seems to have a room for just about every topic imaginable, has a room for FriendFeed questions and best practices. This room, found at http://friendfeed.com/best-practices, is a place for FriendFeed users to go to discuss spammers, how to link to original content sources, and how to interpret "fair use" copyright issues. If you have a question about a specific practice, this room would be the place to check to see if a "best practice" has been worked out.

There are other ways to best use the accounts that you have with these services, besides refraining from sending spam, such as linking original content to its source when possible and not overstepping the bounds of copyright. Some suggestions follow:

▶ **Reuse content**—embed a FriendFeed thread about your library into your Tumblr blog (see, e.g., http://wallacereid .tumblr.com/post/100410348).

▶ **Check out other libraries with accounts**—make sure you know what they are doing in order to determine what is and isn't acceptable for you.

Fair Use Doctrine in Copyright
www.copyright.gov/fls/fl102.html

The fair use doctrine in U.S. copyright law has traditionally been seen as a way for educators to use parts of a copyrighted work in a class, for satire and comedy writers to use parts of a copyrighted work in their social commentary, and for research purposes so that parts of a copyrighted work can be quoted in a research paper—among other, limited uses. The issue comes up frequently when talking about social media, because so much of the content of social networking is user generated and some of that user-generated content may use parts of other works copyrighted by other people. There are no editors or publishers insisting on making sure that copyrighted works are protected in the average social network.

▶ **Make each account part of a conversation**—talk back to those who talk to you, and get involved in other conversations as well.

▶ **Create a policy that defines what is and is not appropriate content for each account**—make sure you are not posting things about your patrons that you would not want them to hear.

▶ CREATE MULTIPLE MICROBLOGGING ACCOUNTS

Creating multiple accounts in Twitter is one way to keep all of your announcements and events going to the people who are most interested in them. You can create a teen account, a bookmobile account, and a general library account and have each of them send out information that is relevant to that audience. If you decide to do this, try using a client that makes managing multiple accounts easier than the standard Twitter Web-based client does. Two that are popular are Splitweet and TwitIQ.

Splitweet bills itself as a "multi-account manager and brand monitor" (http://splitweet.com). It provides tools to keep an eye on more than one account, as well as posting and managing friends, through one single sign-on. Instead of signing on to Twitter multiple times to check and send tweets, you can sign into all of your accounts using Splitweet and view them through its interface. There are other features, most notably the brand monitoring, which does searches for your "brand" name and displays the results for you in the Splitweet Web page.

TwitIQ is very similar, though it focuses on just managing multiple accounts and doesn't have the same sort of extra features that Splitweet does. TwitIQ has positioned itself as a "smarter Twitter web application" (http://twitiq.com), and it focuses on adding value to your Twitter accounts by presenting the same information you can get through a single Twitter account Web page more intelligently—and by supporting multiple accounts per log-in. Either of these sites will help you keep on top of multiple Twitter accounts, which will enable you to target your tweets more precisely.

Some third-party applications such as Tweetdeck support multiple accounts. You may want to be careful about trying to manage multiple accounts, no matter what third-party service you use, though, because it is very easy to post something to a work account that you thought was going to go to a personal account.

For more tips on using Twitter, go to the source and follow @Twitter_Tips, a regularly updated Twitter stream of tips for getting the most out of your Twitter account(s). Other tip collections are also available. One of the best is the TwitIQ blog (www.twitip.com).

Enterprise Tweeting

Because libraries are organizations, some of the tips out there for best practices in using Twitter for businesses can also be applied to us. The Devon Group (http://blog.devongroup.com) has put together a list of 12 tips for enterprise, or business, use of Twitter that are particularly applicable to libraries (http://blog.devongroup.com/?p=523):

1. Understand that it is a commitment.
2. Be prepared to control your message and your brand.
3. Determine company spokespeople (or organizational spokespeople, in the case of libraries).
4. Establish best practices.

5. Have a communication plan (perhaps as part of an overall social software strategy guide).

6. Establish a social media policy (see the discussion of the social software strategy guide in Chapter 4).

7. Learn the lingo.

8. Take advantage of Twitter tools.

9. Join the conversation.

10. Monitor your corporate brand.

11. Monitor your competition (or your cooperative partners—though keeping an eye on local bookstores, Internet-enabled cafés, and any other businesses that do the same things you do might not be a bad idea, too).

12. Conduct an analysis of your efforts (be sure to check out the measuring success information in Chapter 6!).

There is more information on just how to carry out each of these tips right here in this book—you may want to keep a copy of this list close at hand as you begin your social software endeavors and refer to the specific sections of the book for more information on just how to incorporate each of these best practices into your own efforts.

Finally, a tip that I think is essential to successful use of these social software tools is to keep current on not only what people are using but also how they are using it. Add some blog-reading time to your schedule, and keep track of the latest developments in third-party applications, best practices, and tips for usage for each of the services that you use.

▶ COMMENT AND POST OFTEN ON LIFESTREAMING ACCOUNTS

FriendFeed

The number one piece of advice for a productive FriendFeed account is to comment on other people's streams. FriendFeed's FOAF (Friend of a Friend) feature, which displays not only a user's friends but also the posts of their friends on which they have commented, means that if you comment on a post, not only will all of your friends see your comments, but all of the original poster's friends will as well. It is a great way to get more people subscribing to your lifestream and, consequently, made aware of what your library or organization is doing. Be sure, however, to make your comments relevant and not always just about you and your organization—see the discussion on spamming that comes up later!

Add as much of your activity as possible to your FriendFeed stream. The idea behind a lifestreaming service is to aggregate *everything* that you do under one single service. The more you pull into FriendFeed, the better chances you will have of other users becoming aware of all of the cool things that your library or organization does. Do be careful about redundant information, though. Many people have their Twitter accounts set up to feed into their Facebook status updates, then have both fed into FriendFeed—this causes everything posted on Twitter to appear on FriendFeed twice. FriendFeed's very granular options for what gets included in your lifestream will be a big help here. Just go into any of the services that you are pulling in (through the "Settings" link below your name) as if you were editing them and use the check boxes to fine-tune what does and does not get sent to FriendFeed. With the level of control that FriendFeed offers, you should be able to control your lifestream very effectively.

Tumblr

One of the best things you can do with your Tumblr blog (or any blog, for that matter) is to post often. This will not only improve the chances of people subscribing to your tumblog but it will also improve your rankings in search engines, making your tumblog much more easily findable.

Because Tumblr allows you to pull only five external streams of information into your tumblog, you want to be selective about what you offer. Make sure you are not importing redundant information from multiple sources, and also make sure that you are getting a good cross-section of what your organization is doing.

► MANAGE INFORMATION OVERLOAD

Information overload is a common problem for people when they first come into the world of microblogging and lifestreaming. Of course, if people are actually streaming their lives—even just their online lives—you will find more information than can be reasonably dealt with. The tips in this section will help you overcome some of the information overload that comes with Twitter and FriendFeed.

Twitter

One great application for managing information through Twitter is Tweetdeck. As mentioned earlier, Tweetdeck recently began supporting multiple accounts, so you can use a single desktop client to manage all of your library's accounts. This helps to keep all of your information in one place so that you don't have to bounce between Web sites and desktop applications to get updates—it's all happening right there inside of a single application and available with a single glance.

Tweetdeck also gives you the ability to create groups of friends so that you can monitor some friends (connected locals) more closely than you might monitor other friends (other libraries that are not in your general area). Because Tweetdeck offers multiple columns of information, you can put the groups that you want to follow closely on the left side (always visible) and keep less important updates confined to right-side columns that may or may not be visible all the time—depending on the width of your monitor and resolution of your screen.

Making a group is easy, once you have Tweetdeck installed and your account(s) all set up:

1. Press the "Group" button at the top of the Tweetdeck application.
2. Type in a name for the group.
3. Click on the check box next to the name of everyone you want to include in that particular group (from a list of all of the Twitter accounts you follow).

That is all there is to it. Once you have the group made (see Figure 5.1), you can click on the arrows below each column to move them either to the right or to the left so that your most important groups are found at the left, with less important groups on the right (the side that will get cut off on smaller monitors).

▶ Figure 5.1: Tweetdeck Group Screenshot

Another application that can help with information overload is Seesmic (http://seesmic.com). Seesmic also has support for multiple accounts and multiple columns to help sort out accounts and groups that you would like to follow more closely. Most of the desktop applications that are currently available and that will support Twitter have features that many of you will find very helpful in controlling the information streams that Twitter and other social networks produce.

Finally, remember that you don't have to read every single post made by every single friend in order to keep up. Information overload can be handled simply by remembering that this is a river of information—you are not supposed to drink it all in, just reach in occasionally and take a "drink" of the information sliding by. Most of the time, if there is something important going on, you will find out about it because multiple friends will be talking about it and it will come up repeatedly. Otherwise, make sure you keep up with replies that go directly to you and to your Direct Messages, and check on the other stuff as you have the time.

FriendFeed

In FriendFeed, the Web application itself gives you an excellent tool to reduce information overload—the list. Creating lists and segregating people into them is almost necessary to an effective use of FriendFeed, especially since the site started doing real-time updates instead of waiting for the user to refresh the page. This means that as comments are posted, the page moves, and you can easily lose your place in your reading if you are not careful! Don't forget, too, that you can pause this activity by clicking the button at the top right of the page that looks like a VCR pause control (see Figure 5.2).

FriendFeed is so popular and there are so many posts that come through the service that it is very easy to be completely overwhelmed by the sheer number of posts and pictures and links that your friends are making available to you through the service. Creating a new friend list is easy—just click the link on the page that lists all of your friends to create a list, and then start putting different people in different lists. Keep your "home" list (the one that automatically loads when you first log on to FriendFeed) clear of

▶ Figure 5.2: FriendFeed's Pause Button

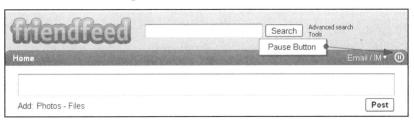

everything but the essentials. These essentials will differ, depending on how you are using the service. These are examples of home lists:

- ▶ **Local News Provider**—just put local friends in your home list and keep all others in separate lists that you can visit as time allows.
- ▶ **Library World Networking**—just put library people in your home list so that you can keep up with what their libraries are doing and join in the library-land conversations that are going on.
- ▶ **Conversational Platform**—keep just the people who are going to help you create and sustain interesting and relevant conversations about your library, your local area, or your particular subject specialty in your home list (be prepared to read this one obsessively so that you can join conversations while they are still happening!).

Manage Followers and Friends

I mentioned earlier that deciding who to follow is something that your organization will have to do on its own. Everyone has different ideas about who to follow and friend for each service. Once you start following people, you can keep lists of who you are following by using any of the backup services mentioned earlier. This is a list of folks who are interested enough in your organization to agree to get your tweets or FriendFeed comments—it's an important list to have!

Besides keeping track of friends, however, you will also want to go through the list periodically and cull out any who are no longer effective for your purposes. Sometimes accounts are created for single-purpose events. After the event is over, the account just sits in your followers list, making it harder to determine who is actually interested in your information. Spammers can occasionally slide into an organization's follower list, too. Again, different organizations have different takes on this issue, but most seem to try to keep spammers from following them, figuring that they do not want to provide any sort of link to that spammer, even if it is from the followers page on their Twitter or FriendFeed account.

▶ AVOID SOCIAL NETWORK SPAMMING

The community seriously frowns on social network spamming, just as it does on e-mail or blog comment spamming. Spam is not just commercial pitches for products sent out indiscriminately to others. In social networking, it results from users who use the service for their own promotion, even if they aren't a commercial organization or business. Spam, in social networks, is also shameless self-promotion! This is why, when I discuss best practices in this book, I often suggest for the best use of a Twitter, FriendFeed, or Tumblr account that you regularly pass along other people's information (retweeting) and post about what other organizations and people are doing in your area. Pointing out what others are accomplishing is not just good karma, it also keeps your fellow microbloggers and lifestreamers from considering you to be a spammer.

Of course, as with all things Internet, there are spammers in Twitter and FriendFeed that you have to watch out for. Both services have an option to block individual users. If you use this feature you can keep spammy accounts from showing up in your friends/followers lists.

Blocking in Twitter

To block a spammer in Twitter, go to the spammer's Twitter profile page and click the link in the "Actions" section of the page on the right sidebar. This will stop the user from showing up in your followers section, and it will keep the user from ever trying to follow you—from that account—again.

Blocking in FriendFeed

FriendFeed has the same option in nearly the same place. Go to the spammer's profile page, and, directly across from the "Subscribe" button, to the right, is a "Block This User" link. This will keep the spammer from resubscribing to your feed.

▶ KEEP UP WITH THE LINGO

Keeping up with the words spawned by the users of Twitter is a full-time job itself. I have defined many of the more common words you will see throughout this book, but if you run into a word that is not familiar, use the Twittonary (www.twittonary.com) to find the meaning of words such as these:

- ▶ **adventuritter**: An adventurous Twitterer.
- ▶ **Blackbird**: A Twitter client for BlackBerry smartphones.
- ▶ **Celebritytweet**: Stalk or follow celebrities on Twitter as they tweet in real-time.
- ▶ **drive-by-tweet**: A quick post in between tasks.
- ▶ **EM/eml**: Shorthand for e-mail.
- ▶ **Fail Whale**: A drawing illustrated by Yiying Lu displayed as a method of informing Twitter users that Twitter is d-o-w-n. There is even a Fail Whale Fan Club.
- ▶ **Geotwitter**: Tracks the geographic location of recent tweets.
- ▶ **HAND**: Have a nice day (acronym).
- ▶ **IRL**: In real life (acronym).
- ▶ **JK or j/k**: Just kidding.
- ▶ **K**: Shorthand for OK.
- ▶ **lmk**: Shorthand for let me know.
- ▶ **mistweet**: A tweet one later regrets.
- ▶ **neweeter**: New tweeter.
- ▶ **occasionitter**: Occasional tweeter.
- ▶ **peeps**: Shorthand for people.
- ▶ **Qwitter**: A tool used to catch when people quit following you.

▶ **Repeatweet**: Resending a tweet (aka "repeated tweet"), just in case anyone missed it. Especially helpful to others when your tweet includes information about natural disasters, health crises, or other important issues . . . or if it was sent in the middle of the night and some followers won't have read it.

▶ **sweeple**: Sweet Twitter people.

▶ **twaggle**: A gaggle of Twitter followers.

▶ **W00t**: An expression of joy and excitement.

▶ **ykyat**: Shorthand for "you know you're addicted to."

▶ **ztwitt**: Tweet very quickly.

The Twitter community coins new words every day. Do not be afraid to ask if someone uses a term with which you are not yet familiar. You will be helping others who are reading the conversation when you get an answer!

Twitter is also, because of its short-posting nature, a natural place to use "text speak." Text speak is made up of abbreviations and phonetic spellings that shorten the number of letters required to get an idea across. They are very popular with texters. The fact that you have a limited number of characters for texting makes abbreviations and other tricks to shorten text very useful. You may see some of the same text speak abbreviations used in Twitter, because many people who text frequently are also Twitter users, so being familiar with text abbreviations will be helpful. There is a comprehensive list of abbreviations at Netlingo (www.netlingo .com/acronyms.php—not all of the abbreviations are "safe for work," however, so visit the page at your own risk), which lists pretty much every abbreviation and text speak short code ever seen (or at least that is what it seems like). Some of the abbreviations will not make sense unless you realize that some of them have traveled over to the text format from the Instant Messaging and chatting world. These are some of the common abbreviations used on Twitter:

▶ **LOL**: Laugh out loud.

▶ **ROTFL**: Rolling on the floor laughing.

- ▶ **MPOW**: My place of work.
- ▶ **MFPOW**: My former place of work.
- ▶ **R**: Are.
- ▶ **@**: At.
- ▶ **BF or b/f**: Boyfriend.
- ▶ **GF or g/f** : Girlfriend.
- ▶ **SO**: Significant other.
- ▶ **srsly**: Seriously.

Hashtags

In Chapter 3, I mentioned hashtags as a way to force a "group" in Twitter. There are other ways to use the hashtag, however, that make Twitter a powerhouse for keeping track of conversations and trends in the online world. You can keep track of hashtags using a search in a desktop application like Tweetdeck, or you can use Twitter's built-in search to keep track of hashtags on the fly. Tweetdeck allows you to create a column for a search term and is a great way to keep track of hashtags that last for a few days, such as a conference hashtag. If you just want a quick look at a particular hashtag, though, you can do a search on Twitter's search page and see the results for that hashtag in real time as they are being posted (or shortly thereafter, depending on the server load that Twitter is experiencing). If you want to keep track of a hashtag for a longer period of time, without using a desktop application, you can do a search and copy the RSS feed for that search into your feed reader (see Figure 5.3).

▶ Figure 5.3: Tweetdeck Displaying a Hashtag Column

▶6

MEASURES OF SUCCESS

▶ **Monitor Microblogging Metrics**
▶ **Monitor Lifestreaming Metrics**

Once you have your accounts set up and have started to use them, measure their success. With a traditional Web site, you would use visitor metrics from the Web logs to determine how many people are visiting the site and if it is successful. Web 2.0 applications, however, are different. They encourage more than just passive visits, so the metrics you use to measure the success of the microblogging or lifestreaming sites that you use need to take in to account more than just visits—you want people to interact with the content, not just consume it passively. You can measure the effectiveness of your efforts in many different ways. You can determine how many people subscribe to your account to get a sense of how far your message is spreading, or you can determine how many people are commenting on your posts to get a sense of the kind of community you are building. Each metric that is available will tell you a little something different about how people are using your accounts and whether or not the message that you are putting out there is getting to the folks who need to hear it.

The tools I mention in this chapter are the technological methods for finding the effectiveness of your Web 2.0 efforts, but there are also nontechnological means for getting this information, too. Ask people when they come to your programs where they heard about them. Newspapers, radio, Twitter, blog, or word of mouth are all ways that you can advertise, and the best way to find out which is working best is to ask. Many times patrons will mention where they heard about a program when they are asking the front desk staff for more information—ask the folks who work those desks to keep track of how often patrons say that they read about a program on the Tumblr blog or saw a mention of it on Twitter.

Comments are a special case. The vast majority of patrons who subscribe to one of your communication channels, such as your Tumblr blog, will never post a comment—most people just do not bother to comment on something that they have read. Because of this, most people do not consider comments (or @replies on Twitter) to be an effective measurement tool of how engaged your audience is. Be careful if you decide to use comments to determine the success of your new Twitter, Tumblr, or FriendFeed venture. Of course, if you post something that is very controversial, you may get a bunch of comments on that one post—but you will have to decide if you really want to create controversy just to get responses from your readers.

A lack of comments does not mean that your tumblog or FriendFeed account is a failure, either. If your goal for the account is primarily information spreading and you have lots of followers, but few comments, that account may still be considered pretty successful, especially if those followers pass that information along to their friends. If your goal in creating the account is to foster conversation, though, you might consider a FriendFeed or Tumblr account that gets no comments or "likes" to be less than successful. Consider this a learning experience, and, because the account was free and you have invested only staff time in it, making the decision to stop investing that staff time could be the way to go for your organization. Most organizations will fall somewhere between. They will have some accounts that are designed to provide information and never ask a question through those channels. Other accounts will be designed to get conversations going and will be geared toward community engagement and creating "action" posts that specifically ask the reader to do something.

▶ MONITOR MICROBLOGGING METRICS

Twitter

Beyond commenting on posts and checking page views, you can view other statistics for your microblogging sites that will give you some idea of how many people use your services. Keep in mind, however, that focusing on just one aspect of your statistics—follower counts, for example—might lead to neglecting other parts of your service that are just as, if not more, important, such as the community that is being built around your account or the reuse of your information. Both of these information points are important to a Web 2.0 initiative.

Several services out there exist just to provide you with a view into your Twitter account's statistics. One, called TweetStats (www .tweetstats.com; see Figure 6.1 for an example stats page from my webgoddess Twitter account), provides graphs of both information about your followers and information about your tweeting habits—how many times you tweet per day, for example.

TweetStats also shows you to whom you reply most often and how you reply—whether through the Web interface, phone (txt), a client such as TwitterFox, or Twhirl or through a status update service such as HelloTxt. From the image in Figure 6.1 of my personal statistics on TweetStats, you can see that I use all methods, but I still use the Web-based interface most often.

Finally, you can use the built-in statistics that Twitter offers—the numbers of followers, Direct Messages, and updates you have made to the service are available from your account's homepage on Twitter. If you are not running a huge marketing campaign, these numbers may be all you need to determine the success of your Twitter account. These statistics alone can answer the big questions:

▶ Is your account growing?

▶ Are you posting often enough to keep people interested but not so often that your people perceive you as a spammer?

▶ Are people using the account—sending you Direct Message questions or using the reply feature to engage your organization in conversation?

You can find the answers to all of these questions on the Twitter site itself, and all of them can give you a good idea of how successful your Twitter account actually is. The statistics provided by

▶ Figure 6.1: TweetStats Graphing My Personal Twitter Account

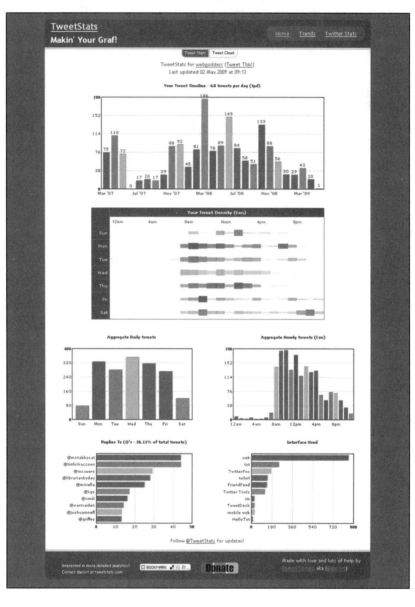

third-party applications like TweetStats or TweepleTwak can give you more detailed information that may come in handy, but the built-in statistics that Twitter provides may be enough for your organization.

Tumblr

Tumblr does not currently have any built-in statistics that you can consult to determine the success of your Tumblr blog, but this does not mean that you have no way of knowing what is happening with your tumblog. You can find out, in graphical form, information about your posting frequency and style with a tool like TumblrStats. Using this tool is simple:

1. Go to www.tumblrstats.com.
2. Enter your Tumblr user name in the text box.
3. View your graphs.

That is all there is to it. The statistics given by this tool are just for what you are doing on the blog, not for who else is visiting the blog or what particular posts they are reading. For that, you can use the free Web site analytics program from Google—Google Analytics (www.google.com/analytics). If you have a Google account, you can use it to sign in to the Google Analytics site and set it up to work with your Tumblr blog:

1. Sign in to Google and go to www.google.com/analytics/provision to set up a new account for analytics.
2. Click the "Sign Up" button.
3. Enter the Tumblog's URL, the name you want to give the account, the location, and the time zone, and then click "Continue."
4. Enter your name and location again, and click "Continue."
5. Agree to the Terms of Service, and click "Create New Account."
6. Copy the code in the box and paste it into the "Description" field in your Tumblr blog. To get to the "Description" field:
   a. Click "Customize" from your blog's homepage (you will see this only when you are signed into the Tumblr site).
   b. Click the "Info" menu at the top of the Customize page.
   c. The "Description" field is the second text box in the drop-down page that appears.
7. Click on "Save Changes," and Google will begin collecting information about your visitors.

FairShare

If you are interested in knowing who is reusing your work, you can go to https://fairshare.attributor.com/fairshare/ to see where your text is showing up on the Web. Just enter the URL of your Tumblr blog's feed and decide how you want to share your work. If you are not interested in licensing your work, choose to have FairShare just show you where your content is going. Create a FairShare account and then choose how you want to receive the feed from your account. Once this is done, FairShare will search the Web for uses of your content, and let you know via its RSS feed where it is and if you are getting proper credit for it. FairShare also includes a service called RevShare that provides some revenue-sharing capabilities for your content. Using RevShare means that you can get advertising revenue from pages that take your full content feed and repost it, as long as they are using a supported advertising network (see the previous URL to find out what networks are supported).

Once you have put the code into your Tumblr blog, you can begin tracking what posts are most popular, where people are coming from when they visit your site, and what kind of search terms they are using to find it.

▶ MONITOR LIFESTREAMING METRICS

FriendFeed's statistics are all right there on the site. If you click on your name and go to your page on the site, you will see a list of stats at the top:

- ▶ **Subscriptions**—how many people you subscribe to.
- ▶ **Subscribers**—how many people subscribe to you.
- ▶ **Comments**—the number of comments you have made (all time).
- ▶ **Likes**—the number of posts you have liked (all time).

You can also get information about how your account is doing via a tool like FeedStats (found at www.feedstats.info), which provides a more detailed view of your FriendFeed account.

No matter how you get your numbers, remember that nothing happens overnight and that nothing happens without a good bit of work being involved. If you start up a Twitter account for your library and expect thousands of followers the next day, you will be disappointed. Start slow, friend those you feel would appreciate your content, post good content, and let people who might not be using the service know that you are there. Each of these steps—for any of the microblogging or lifestreaming applications discussed in this book—will help develop your audience and create a successful and vibrant community online.

RECOMMENDED RESOURCES

▶ PRINT

Cohen, Steven M. 2007. "I Twittered, Then I 'Tumbld'. . . ." *Information Today* 24, no. 5: 20–21. *MasterFILE Premier*, EBSCO*host* (accessed November 22, 2009).

Cohen, Steven M. 2008. "You've Got a Friend (Feed) in Me." *Information Today* 25, no. 7: 17–17. *MasterFILE Premier*, EBSCO*host* (accessed November 22, 2009).

Comm, Joel. 2009. *Twitter Power: How to Dominate Your Market One Tweet at a Time*. New York: Wiley.

Evans, Dave. 2008. *Social Media Marketing: An Hour a Day*. New York: Sybex.

Fitton, Laura, Michael Gruen, and Leslie Poston. 2009. *Twitter for Dummies*. New York: For Dummies.

Hargadon, Steve. 2009. "Microblogging: It's Not Just Twitter." *School Library Journal* 55, no. 2: 15. *MasterFILE Premier*, EBSCO*host* (accessed November 22, 2009).

McFedries, Paul. 2009. *Twitter Tips, Tricks, and Tweets*. New York: Wiley.

Miller, Claire Cain. 2009. "Putting Twitter's World to Use." *New York Times* (April 14): 1. *MasterFILE Premier*, EBSCO*host* (accessed November 22, 2009).

Milstein, Sarah. 2009. "Twitter FOR Libraries (and Librarians)." *Online* 33, no. 2: 34–35. *MasterFILE Premier*, EBSCO*host* (accessed November 22, 2009).

► WEB-BASED

Twitter RSS and API Use Tutorials

Twitter—Tips & Tutorials. Available: www.newwebplatform.com/ tips-and-tutorials/Twitter (accessed November 22, 2009). A list of Twitter help sites that focus on the use of the Twitter API and RSS feeds.

Twitter API Wiki. Available: http://apiwiki.twitter.com (accessed November 22, 2009). The official site with all of the documentation for the Twitter API.

Twitter

Devon Group. Available: http://blog.devongroup.com (accessed November 22, 2009). A blog that contains information on using Twitter for businesses, including some good tips for nonprofit organizations.

Erickson, David. "Twenty-six Twitter Tools to Track Tweets." eStrategy Internet Marketing Blog. Available: e-strategyblog.com/ 2009/02/twenty-six-twitter-tools-to-track-tweets (accessed November 22, 2009).

Hyder, Kenny. "14 Tools of Highly Effective Twitter Users—Kenny Hyder." Available: http://hyder.me/social-media/14-tools-of -highly-effective-twitter-users (accessed November 22, 2009). Hyder is a marketing consultant, photographer, and wine enthusiast.

King, David Lee. "Twitter Explained for Librarians, or 10 Ways to Use Twitter." Available: www.davidleeking.com/2007/03/10/ twtter-explained-for-librarians-or-10-ways-to-use-twitter (accessed November 22, 2009). A post that is somewhat old (it dates from before Twitter had its own search engine) but is still useful in finding ways to use Twitter for your library.

monitter. Available: http://monitter.com (accessed November 22, 2009). A real-time, free widget to monitor the Twitter world based on your keywords.

Owyang, Jeremiah. "Ask Jeremiah: The Comprehensive FAQ Guide to Twitter." Available: www.web-strategist.com/blog/

2009/03/11/ask-jeremiah-comprehensive-faq-guide-to-twitter (accessed November 22, 2009).

Smith, Chris. "Harness the Power of Twitter for Local Marketing." Available: http://searchengineland.com/how-to-use-twitter-for -local-marketing-16809 (accessed November 22, 2009). Search Engine Land: Must Read News about Search Marketing & Search Engines.

TweetScan Data Backup. Available: www.tweetscan.com/data.php (accessed November 22, 2009). A service that backs up tweets, friends, replies, Direct Messages, and followers.

TwiTip blog. Available: www.twitip.com (accessed November 22, 2009). A blog with frequent updates pointing to "TwiTips" (Twitter tips).

Twitter Fan Wiki. "Twitter Etiquette." Available: www.twitter.pbwiki .com/Twitter Etiquette (accessed November 22, 2009).

Twittonary. Available: www.twittonary.com (accessed November 22, 2009). An online Twitter dictionary, useful when you want to look up an abbreviation or a word that you have not yet encountered on the Twitter service.

WeFollow: A User Powered Twitter Directory. http://wefollow .com (accessed November 22, 2009). A directory of Twitter users, although it is not automatic. Twitter users have to add their accounts to be listed, so it is not exhaustive.

Searching Twitter and FriendFeed

Allison, Chris. "Welcome to the Hive Mind; Learn How to Search Twitter." Available: www.twitip.com/welcome-to-the-hive-mind -learn-how-to-search-twitter (accessed November 22, 2009). A post that explains the most useful of Twitter's advanced search operators.

Third-Party Applications for Twitter and FriendFeed

Apps. Available: friendfeed.com/apps (accessed November 22, 2009). A FriendFeed group created to announce—and discuss—new applications for the FriendFeed site. You get not only new application announcements but also reports from people who have used the application and who describe what they do and don't like about the applications. Other social applications are also discussed in this group.

Archivist. Available: http://flotzam.com/archivist (accessed November 22, 2009). A Windows application that runs on your computer and saves your tweets on your local machine.

bit.ly. Available: http://bit.ly (accessed November 22, 2009). A URL shortening service with extra features like URL tracking included.

FriendFeed apps. Available: http://ffapps.com (accessed November 22, 2009). A list of applications that have been compiled and presented for folks to use.

LongURL. Available: http://longurl.org/tools (accessed November 22, 2009). A Firefox extension that expands short URLs so that you know where you are going before you click.

Mashable. "7 Desktop Applications for FriendFeed." Available: http://mashable.com/2008/10/01/desktop-applications-for -friendfeed (accessed November 22, 2009). A roundup of FriendFeed friendly applications, with reviews and notes on how to use each of them.

TweepML. Available: http://tweepml.org/tag/librarian (accessed November 22, 2009). A way to create and share groups of users—predates Twitter's own lists features.

Tweetdeck. Available: www.tweetdeck.com/beta (accessed November 22, 2009). A desktop application that you can install on your computer that will organize several different views of Twitter onto one screen.

Tweetdeck Vimeo Tags. Available: http://vimeo.com/tag :tweetdeck (accessed November 22, 2009). The creators of Tweetdeck upload videos to Vimeo, a video-sharing service, that explain the features of Tweetdeck as they are released. This is a good way to get an overview of how to use the software when you are first trying it out.

Twhirl. Available: www.twhirl.org (accessed November 22, 2009). One of the Twitter/FriendFeed clients that is downloadable and runs on the Adobe Air platform.

Twitter Fan Wiki. Available: http://twitter.pbwiki.com/Apps (accessed November 22, 2009). A list of applications that the fans of Twitter have compiled, including links and descriptions of each program or Web-based service in the categories of desktop apps, Web apps, and mobile apps.

OpenMicroBlogging

OpenMicroBlogging Standard. Available: http://openmicroblogging .org/about (accessed November 22, 2009). An organization creating a standard microblogging protocol to connect various microblogging providers (Twitter, Plurk, Identi.ca, etc.) together.

INDEX

Page numbers followed by the letter "f" indicate figures.

▶

ABOUT THE AUTHOR

Robin Hastings is the Information Technology Manager for the Missouri River Regional Library. In that capacity, she is responsible for the library's network, computers, and Web sites and for training the staff in computer skills. She helped to create the second Library Learning 2.0 program in the country and manages most of the library's social networking accounts. She has worked in libraries for over ten years and is passionate about the unique challenges that libraries face. She takes that passion on the road quite frequently, speaking at conferences from England to Jamaica to all over the United States. She generally talks about teaching librarians how to use social networks, how to reuse data from social networks (and elsewhere) on their Web sites, and what's coming in the next, 3.0, iteration of the Web.

Robin has also written about libraries in the *Library Journal and Computers in Libraries,* and she authored an ALA Library Technology Report on Collaboration 2.0 in May/June of 2009. You can find her as "webgoddess" on most social networks or blogging about technology and libraries at www.rhastings.net.